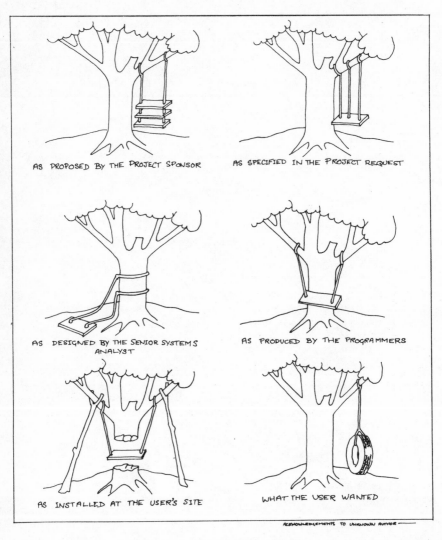

From the *University of London Computer Centre Newsletter* No. 53, March 1973

GUIDE TO
GOOD PROGRAMMING
PRACTICE

THE ELLIS HORWOOD SERIES IN COMPUTERS AND THEIR APPLICATIONS

Series Editor: Brian Meek, Director, Computer Unit, Queen Elizabeth College, University of London

The series aims to provide up-to-date and readable texts on the theory and practice of computing, with particular though not exclusive emphasis on computer applications. Preference is given in planning the series to new or developing areas, or to new approaches in established areas.

The books will usually be at the level of introductory or advanced undergraduate courses. In most cases they will be suitable as course texts, with their use in industrial and commercial fields always kept in mind. Together they will provide a valuable nucleus for a computing science library.

Published and in active publication

INTRODUCTORY ALGOL 68 PROGRAMMING
D. F. BRAILSFORD and A. N. WALKER, Department of Mathematics, University of Nottingham

SOFTWARE ENGINEERING
K. GEWALD, G. HAAKE and W. PFADLER

FUNDAMENTALS OF COMPUTER LOGIC
D. HUTCHISON, Department of Computer Science, University of Strathclyde

INTERACTIVE COMPUTER GRAPHICS IN SCIENCE TEACHING
Edited by J. McKENZIE, Department of Physics and Astronomy, University College, London
L. ELTON, Head of Institute of Educational Technology, University of Surrey
and R. LEWIS, Head of Educational Computing, Chelsea College, University of London

SYSTEMS ANALYSIS AND DESIGN FOR COMPUTER APPLICATIONS
D. MILLINGTON, Department of Computer Science, University of Strathclyde

RECURSIVE FUNCTIONS IN COMPUTER SCIENCE
R. PETER, Professor of Mathematics, Eotvos Lorand University of Budapest

AUTOREGRESSION ALGORITHMS
L. J. SLATER, Department of Applied Economics, University of Cambridge, and H. M. PESARAN, Trinity College, Cambridge

CLUSTER ANALYSIS ALGORITHMS
HELMUT SPATH, Professor of Mathematics, Oldenburg University

GUIDE TO GOOD PROGRAMMING PRACTICE

Editors:

B. L. MEEK, M.Sc.,
Director, Computer Unit,
Queen Elizabeth College,
University of London

and

P. M. HEATH, B.A.,
Programming Manager,
Computer Centre,
Plymouth Polytechnic

ELLIS HORWOOD LIMITED
Publishers   Chichester

Halsted Press: a division of
JOHN WILEY & SONS
New York - Chichester - Brisbane - Toronto

First published in 1980 by
ELLIS HORWOOD LIMITED
Market Cross House, Cooper Street, Chichester, West Sussex, PO19 1EB, England

The publisher's colophon is reproduced from James Gillison's drawing of the ancient Market Cross, Chichester.

Distributors:

Australia, New Zealand, South-east Asia:
Jacaranda-Wiley Ltd., Jacaranda Press,
JOHN WILEY & SONS INC.,
G.P.O. Box 859, Brisbane, Queensland 40001, Australia.

Canada:
JOHN WILEY & SONS CANADA LIMITED
22 Worcester Road, Rexdale, Ontario, Canada.

Europe, Africa:
JOHN WILEY & SONS LIMITED
Baffins Lane, Chichester, West Sussex, England.

North and South America and the rest of the world:
Halsted Press, a division of
JOHN WILEY & SONS
605 Third Avenue, New York, N.Y. 10016, U.S.A.

British Library Cataloguing in Publication Data
    Guide to good programming practice. —
    (Computers and their applications).
    1. Electronic digital computers — Programming
    I. Meek, Brian Lawrence II. Heath, P M
    III. Series
    001.6'42   QA76.6   79-40993
ISBN 0-85312-145-1 (Ellis Horwood Ltd., Publishers)
ISBN 0-470-26869-7 (Halsted Press)
ISBN 0-85312-152-4 (Ellis Horwood Ltd., Publishers) (Student Edition)
Typeset in Press Roman by Ellis Horwood Ltd.
Printed and bound in Great Britain by
W & J Mackay Limited, Chatham

Table of Contents

Chapter 5 Other people

Preface

During an introductory course on computer programming, one's concentration is usually directed towards mastering the features of the programming language used, rather than on wider aspects of the programmer's craft. Similarly, programming manuals and textbooks tend to concentrate on language features. Some do no more than present these, though the better ones also discuss good programming style and methodology. However, for quite understandable reasons they virtually never go beyond those aspects of good programming practice that are directly related to program writing. Too often, people are left to pick up the wider aspects later, by experience, learning on the job, and through informal advice rather than systematic discussion.

This book sets out to present in a straightforward and easily assimilable form all of the main aspects of good programming practice. It is not related to the use of any particular language or machine, though a few examples are given in various well-known languages for the purposes of illustration. It is therefore designed to supplement and not replace the usual kinds of introductory manuals, books, and courses, and to provide a useful source of guidance and reference later, as the newly-fledged programmer begins to put his skills to practical use. Within the space available it has not been possible to cover all techniques; for example, structured programming is discussed in terms mainly of general principles rather than the detailed methodology more appropriate to programming courses; the use of decision tables has been left to more specialized texts; and discussion of correctness proofs of programs has been omitted, reluctantly, as being still an area of research and experiment rather than of established technique. Suggestions for further reading are included as an appendix, and readers are strongly advised to use this to follow up topics of particular interest or relevance.

The authors have between them had many decades of experience of programming, in a variety of contexts; though most are now working in educational establishments, several have had experience outside in industry and commerce, and still have contacts there. As well as providing their own contributions, the authors have read and sent in comments upon the drafts of others; the editors would like to thank them for this (especially David Hill), and also for cheerfully accepting editorial changes, sometimes substantial, made as a result of such comments or for reasons of continuity. In addition, Hushang Balyuzi and Steve Lackovic of the Physics Department, Queen Elizabeth College, suggested a considerable number of improvements to Section 4.5. Thanks are are also due to Miss Gim Tan of the Computer Unit, Queen Elizabeth College, for performing a great deal of typing, copying, and other necessary secretarial work. Finally, we wish to thank Patrick Gibbins and the editor of the *University of London Computer Centre Newsletter* for their permission to reproduce the 'swing' cartoon, which captures more neatly than anything else we know the essence of what the business is all about.

March 1979   Brian Meek
                                                             Patricia Heath

Notes on Contributors

Dr MICHAEL CLARKE is a lecturer in Computer Science at Queen Mary College, London.

PATRICIA HEATH is Programming Manager at the Computer Centre, Plymouth Polytechnic.

CAROL HEWLETT is in charge of the advisory service of the Computer Unit, London School of Economics.

PAUL HIDE is Senior Programmer in charge of the advisory service of the Computer Unit, Queen Elizabeth College, London.

Dr I. D. HILL is a statistician employed by the Medical Research Council and senior Honorary Secretary of the Royal Statistical Society during 1978-80.

BRIAN MEEK is Director of the Computer Unit, Queen Elizabeth College, London.

RICHARD OVERILL is an advisory programmer in the Computer Unit, King's College, London.

NICHOLAS RUSHBY is manager of the Applications Programming Group in the Computer Centre, Imperial College, London.

JOHN STEEL is head of Applications at the Computer Centre, Queen Mary College, London.

MARTIN WILSON is a divisional manager at Logica Ltd.

CHAPTER 1

Strategy and Design

People commonly start their programming career by learning a programming language, usually through an introductory course. Inevitably, in the early stages their dominant concern is with mastering the language constructs and the fundamentals of breaking down and reorganizing a problem into a form to which those constructs can be applied. Some introductory courses concentrate so much on the language and how to use it to express the solutions to problems, that virtually everything else is excluded, though the better ones do stress general principles, such as structured programming techniques, which are not language-specific or problem-specific. It is usually only later, when one has started programming seriously (either through becoming a professional programmer, or because programming is an important adjunct to other work) that the realization gradually dawns that there is a good deal more to being a programmer (whether a professional or a serious amateur) than simply coding. Indeed, for some the realization seems never to dawn at all.

The object of this book is to present, in a compact and assimilable form, the essentials of what is involved in being a serious and competent programmer, whether or not professionally employed as such, seen through the eyes of people each of whom has been active in the field for several years. The emphasis throughout is on essential principles, detail being left for further reading except for purposes of illustration. Not everything will be directly relevant to every individual or to every programming problem, but any could become relevant with a change of job or the start of a new project. Some of the advice may strike you as trite and obvious; if so, well and good. If some of it helps you to recognize, formulate, and rationalize things you already know into a coherent 'philosophy of programming', even better. If anything strikes you as a new idea worth considering (or possibly as a brilliant flash of enlightenment!), that is best of all.

The book is organized into five chapters. The ordering is logical, but it is not the only possible logical ordering. The first chapter deals with the question of overall approach, and then goes on to discuss principles of program design — though not immediately, because this is preceded by a discussion of the use of the literature, program packages and so on. 'Re-inventing the wheel' can occur in any human activity, and in programming it is rife; thus the purpose of this section is to stress that it is always worth checking to see if the program you want, or a substantial part of it, already exists. Many programs have been written when equally good or better ones to do the same job have been available 'off the shelf' — something which is forgivable for practice as a part of one's training, but not otherwise.

Chapter 2 deals with actual program writing, including programming languages (with a special section on the tricky question of language standardization), input-output considerations, and of course structured programming. Chapter 3 continues with the theme of structured programming in relation to program development, including error prevention, debugging, and improvement of performance. Chapter 4 takes this last question further, by discussing the special problems which can arise in certain kinds of application. Finally, Chapter 5 deals with an area sometimes overlooked completely — the programmer's relation-ship with and responsibilities to other people who may be involved, including the important matter of documentation.

1.1 APPROACHING THE PROBLEM

It is a common experience, for a person on an introductory training course, to find that his program does not behave as expected, and that this can be traced to the fact that, when he wrote the program, he did not fully understand the requirements of the problem it was supposed to solve. Thus the first piece of advice to be offered may appear to fall into the 'trite and obvious' category — make sure you understand the problem before you start to write the program.

However, though it may be trite and obvious, it is still worth stating. One of the most frequent misconceptions about programming is that the first thing one does is sit down at a terminal, or write one's name on a coding sheet, and start writing program text. In fact, what happens before one gets to this stage is often of crucial importance to the success of the project.

Beginners are often encouraged to 'dive in head first' in this way when they are on an initial course, partly to engender confidence, and partly to provide motivation. It must be stressed that exercises set at the beginning of such courses are necessarily of a predigested form, where the problems are carefully chosen so that potential difficulties, other than those which the exercises are explicitly designed to test, are either avoided or were non-existent in the first place. Unfortunately, the impression is sometimes given that all programming is like that. This is very far from the truth; in any realistic project the likelihood that it will occur is almost zero.

The beginner on such a course should think of himself as a baby being fed carefully selected, easily digestible food, but must expect in time to cut his teeth on tougher (but more interesting) food which will need a fair bit of chewing, and eventually to move on to taking a hand in the preparation before even being able to sit down and eat.

One feature of such predigested exercises is that they are usually very precisely specified, as well as being simple. The serious problems that have to be tackled later are seldom so simple, and may not be so precisely specified. If the problem is of your own devising (typically if you are a 'serious amateur' needing to write a program in the course of another piece of work) the important thing is to formulate as clearly as possible what you want to achieve before starting to design a program. One method is to put down on paper a specification of what is to be done — the starting data, what is to be achieved, the means of achieving it, any constraints (such as of time or money) which have to be satisfied, and so on. This in itself often helps to clarify the mind, but it is often useful to give this specification to a colleague with suitable background knowledge, and ask him to see if he can understand it or can find any flaws, ambiguities, or omissions.

If the project is not of your own devising (typically, if you are employed as a programmer by some organization) it may be presented to you in any form from general verbal instructions to a complete written specification. If you do have a specification, it is essential at this stage to read it thoroughly and make sure that you understand every part of it. If there is anything which you do not understand, ask for clarification. Resist the temptation to try to avoid 'loss of face' or appearing stupid, in the hope that all will become clear later. Whatever the risk of this may be, it is far less serious than the consequences of producing something based on misunderstanding. Similarly, if the specification is not very precise, or is incomplete, or not written down at all, it is strongly recommended that you write your own precise specification, and seek confirmation that it does represent what you are supposed to be doing. If more people are involved than just the programmer and the person who wants the program, everyone needs to have the same understanding of what is being done, and in any case it is, once again, worth obtaining an independent opinion on whether the specification is complete and unambiguous. When it first appeared, the 'swing' cartoon which forms the frontispiece of this book must have struck a responsive chord in many experienced programmers who had learned these lessons the hard way.

The second piece of advice, which may not be quite so obvious, is to take a complete view of the whole project at the outset, not just the question of program design. The preamble to this chapter referred to the logical ordering of topics in this book, which does to some extent reflect the sequential progression of a project through program design, program writing, and program development to the production of a complete, fully documented final product. However, it by no means reflects the order in which the programmer has to consider the various factors. To take an extreme example, documentation is something which must start right at the beginning (with the project specification) and be maintained throughout; the topic is placed near the end only because documentation cannot be completed until the rest of the project is completed. However, all the various stages are intimately interconnected. Program design and writing must be done with the later necessity for debugging borne in mind. Any of the special problems discussed in Chapter 4, such as long or continuous running, will affect the algorithmic design at an early stage. The analysis of the requirements of the problem may influence matters like the choice of programming language or of input-output media; but equally, the availability or not of certain languages or certain equipment can influence algorithmic design. Such points will become apparent in the ensuing pages.

This is why taking a complete overview of a project is so essential, to try to evaluate which of the factors are likely to be dominant, and the relative priorities of the criteria which will be used to judge between the various options which may arise. Furthermore, these matters should be kept in mind throughout, as the project progresses. It may be that these initial judgements will turn out to be faulty, or that they will be rendered invalid by changing circumstances, but this will by no means always be the case, and is no excuse for failing to make them.

The IBM slogan 'THINK' is a standing joke in the computer world, but this does not alter the fact that it is extremely good advice. What we have been saying in this section is that, however short the deadlines and whatever the pressures may be, the time you spend thinking about the project as a whole, taking a complete overview, getting it in perspective, will virtually always be time well spent. Because of the way it aids this process of understanding, we have also recommended discussing the project with someone else. The question of seeking specific help during the progress of a project is dealt with later, but a few more remarks are worth making here. At this initial stage it is the fact of the discussion which is important — provided it is a genuine discussion and aimed at analysis, rather than being intended to impress — and the particular person with whom the discussion is held is, in a way, secondary. It may be a colleague, or the client, or your boss, any of whom may be able to contribute helpful advice or information, but for the purpose of clarifying your own thoughts, anyone willing to listen will do, as long-suffering marital or premarital partners of successful programmers will testify. If the worst comes to the worst and no-one will listen, it is even worth imagining you are describing your project to an audience of sceptical experts — though remember to try not to disturb your family or landlady or neighbours in the process!

Whatever you do, however, make sure you think the project through as far as you can before starting work on it; even if the deadline is only two hours away, at least spend ten minutes thinking, before sitting down at your terminal or your coding pad.

Brian Meek

1.2 USING THE LITERATURE

Since the first essential in any project is to think, to consider carefully what is to be done, to ensure that the problem to be solved is fully understood, any aids to such understanding are important. The value has already been pointed out of discussing the problem with others, such as the future user of the program, the project leader, and other team members. Furthermore, full understanding of the problem does not necessarily mean that a solution will immediately present itself, nor that the full implications in the computing sense — for example, what kind and size of resources will be needed — will be immediately clear.

The first use of the literature in a project is therefore commonly for background reading in the area of the problem, both to gain fuller understanding and to find clues towards methods of solution. As the programmer's understanding deepens, through such discussions and reading, possible methods will begin to present themselves, either as direct suggestions or as ideas of his own, and some will become clearer favourites than others because they seem more appropriate to the particular problem or more suitable to the computing facilities available. But before becoming too enamoured of a particular method, it is essential to take stock, and consider what options are available.

At this stage it is worth noting that in some cases a project may be presented to you with a ready-made solution, perhaps provided by the project leader or the future user. If it comes from the project leader he is probably right (and if he is wrong it may be difficult to tell him!). Nevertheless, if you want to do a good professional job it is still your responsibility to convince yourself that this is the right solution, or one of the right solutions. A good project leader will, as a matter of course, explain not only the method but the reasons for choosing it. If the solution comes from the user, the situation may be still more delicate; but again it is your responsibility to convince yourself that it is correct. One example, which will be used again shortly, is that the user may ask for a particular statistical test to be performed on his data; unless he is a professional statistician the validity of the test for the data should be checked, if possible. One of the authors, when a very 'green' beginner, was given an algorithm to code, without being told the problem which the algorithm was designed to solve. Many man-weeks of effort and much machine time were wasted on variations which never produced results to the user's liking; eventually our green young programmer, fast learning his professionalism the hard way, plucked up courage to ask what the algorithm was supposed to do. Once he was told, a correct algorithm was found, coded, and run within a few hours. However, most of the time the problem will not be that the method is actually wrong, but that it is not the best for the particular equipment or mode of use because the user is not expert in computing. Whatever the situation, however, the general rule is the same: don't accept any proposed method on trust; check it out for yourself as far as you can, and particularly be on the lookout for concealed or implicit assumptions which may not be valid.

Once the problem is well understood and the preferred method of solution decided, the time has come to search the literature again. This is because three possibilities exist for the provision of the actual program:

(1) A program or package may already exist which could be used;
(2) There may be modules available, for example in a subroutine library or as part of a program for a related problem, which can be incorporated in the required program;
(3) The whole program may have to be written from scratch.

Far too many programmers, especially beginners and occasional programmers who write programs for their own use as part of other work, take it for granted that option 3 will be used, and never think of searching the literature, both the program libraries which almost all computer installations have or the literature of the subject, for a suitable existing program which can be taken over or modified. This may partly be through ignorance of the vast extent of the literature of this kind which now exists; it may be through an unfounded belief that 'my problem must be unique' or (even less likely to be tenable) that 'whatever anyone else has done, I can do it better'; it may simply be that they enjoy writing programs and would rather do that than take over what someone else has done. Even professional programmers are not wholly immune; there is what is known as the 'not invented here' syndrome which leads computer installations to develop large pieces of software like operating systems or compilers or payroll packages although apparently adequate ones already exist.

The existence of programs or modules relevant to the problem does not, however, automatically mean that they should be used; whether you choose to adopt or adapt existing software, or to write everything yourself, you must ensure that you will be using valid, up-to-date techniques, and ones which can be implemented on your computer — criteria which again involve some reference to the literature. A program based on a method of solution inapplicable in the particular circumstances is useless, whether written by oneself or obtained from elsewhere. On occasion it is worth compromising slightly upon the ideal method to gain the benefit of being able to use a standard package, but only when it is certain that the method is still valid and the losses are unimportant compared with the gains. For instance, mention has already been made of statistics, where there are very stringent requirements for the application of given techniques to data. To take a simple example, the χ^2 test can be applied only to data consisting of frequencies, not to measurements or percentages; so when asked to provide a program to assess the probability of a given distribution being produced randomly, it is essential, before using a χ^2 test, to establish that the data is of the kind required and that the test will not be applied inappropriately.

With criteria of this kind there is little or no scope for compromise. Such situations arise across the whole range of computer applications, from numerical algorithms used in scientific computations to the sorting and searching and file-handling techniques needed for many commercial programs. The literature available must be used to check that the method being used is legitimate.

An added complication is that new ways of solving particular problems are becoming available almost daily. They cover both the algorithms which might be used, and features of modern machine architecture which can be exploited. It is thus necessary to refer to recent relevant publications, technical and/or academic, to glean information on the most up-to-date approaches.

Quite apart from acquiring such information, all the relevant facts about the equipment and facilities available must be ascertained. For example, if a particular language is not available on your machine, a package in that language will be of no practical use, however appropriate it may be for your project. As will be discussed later (Section 5.2) your program advisory service, documentation officer, operations supervisor, or other responsible person will be able to provide detailed help with the facilities available, and much of the literature you will need you will be able to obtain from them. What is available will range from an introductory guide to the installation, to the manufacturer's manuals on the hardware, operating system etc. Once you have got to the stage of having absorbed the relevant information both from the literature of the subject and from the documentation describing the facilities available, you are in a position to start work on the actual solution to your problem.

Pause at this stage, and check on the programming and documentation standards required of you; these should themselves be documented somewhere. These standards should be applied and adhered to right from the beginning. Even if there are no specific local requirements, good programming practice requires documentation to be produced satisfying certain standards, and anyone who wishes to become a really good programmer will cultivate the habit of always documenting his programs, even if only for his own use. Again, there is literature available to advise you; the general principles, and guidance on where to find detailed standards, are discussed in Section 5.1.

Everything so far has referred to the use of the literature before the project fully gets under way in terms of program design and writing, or alternatively testing an existing package. The ideal situation to be in is to have a program already available, exactly meeting the requirements of the project, well documented, thoroughly tested, and already implemented at your installation. Put like that, it sounds impossibly utopian; but in a good many standard areas of computer application there are such programs, and an increasing amount of literature describing them is available. Most computer manufacturers provide applications packages of various kinds which will be listed in some 'software directory'; this should be available in your installation even if every item in it is not 'up' on your local machine. Even if the ideal is not quite reached, it should be easy to find out if your installation can and will put up for you the particular program you need. Such directories from the manufacturer are commonly supplemented by software exchange directories available through user groups, which nowadays exist for most common machine ranges. Again, some of this software may already have been obtained by your installation. Two warnings are needed here, however: the documentation of such software may not always be quite up to the highest professional standards, and the level of support which can be obtained if difficulties are encountered may be less than that expected for manufacturer-supplied software.

In addition to such machine-oriented sources, there are also subject-oriented sources. Some, like SPSS in statistics or COMPAY in the commercial world, are packages written in some widely-available language or languages, like Fortran or Cobol, and often implemented on many machine ranges. Those produced by professional programmers, for example by software houses, can be expected to be fully documented and tested. Others appear in technical and academic journals or in conference proceedings, for example as appendices listing programs used in the research described in the paper. These again (though this is by no means always the case) may fall short of professional standards of documentation. Once again, the only rule for the true professional is never to take anything on trust, whether it comes as an unannotated printout from an obvious (computing) amateur, or with the highest credentials from the most eminent computer scientists or with the guarantee of the computer manufacturer.

If no complete package can be found which provides exactly what you want, the possibility still remains that at least existing modules can be incorporated into the final program. As well as abstracting these from packages, it is possible to obtain them from module or subroutine libraries, or from sources which tend to supply such modules rather than complete programs. Libraries such as the NAG library (for numerical algorithms) allow you to use well-written algorithms as part of a program tailored to your particular project; journals such as *Communications of the A. C. M.*, *Computer Journal* and *Applied Statistics* regularly publish algorithms, and it is becoming increasingly common for textbooks in particular subject areas to include specifications in some form or another (usually a listing in some commonly available language) of important algorithms. The same general principles apply as with complete programs: make sure the algorithm is really the one you want, and verify that it really does what is claimed.

Despite the proliferation of program and module libraries and of published algorithms generally, inevitably situations will arise where there is no alternative to writing your own complete program. The project may be especially unusual, or there may be hardware or software difficulties which prevent the use of an existing package or module. The succeeding sections of this book are especially concerned with this, but it is worth noting that, again, the literature needs to be consulted, especially the manuals of your installation describing languages, hardware, and other facilities available. Programming languages, for example, come in a variety of dialects, and there may be particular quirks or extensions in the version at your installation which either can be exploited or, if your program is intended to be transportable elsewhere, should be avoided. The sticky question of programming language standards (which of course applies equally in the opposite direction when obtaining existing programs from elsewhere, as envisaged above) is discussed in Section 2.3, and appears again in Section 5.3. Even more implementation-specific are matters like file handling and character manipulation. All this needs to be looked up in the literature, noted where relevant, and taken into account.

In the typical nontrivial project, the literature to be studied can appear extremely daunting (though of course much of the knowledge gained, such as that concerning facilities available at your installation, can be carried forward from project to project). Nevertheless, without familiarity with or at least awareness of all the relevant information available in the literature, a thoroughly competent and professional job cannot be guaranteed.

Patricia Heath

1.3 THE DESIGN OF ALGORITHMS

Introduction
The programs that one writes as exercises during the early stages of a programming course represent simple tasks expressed in the unfamiliar medium of a programming language. The object of these exercises is to help the beginner to master the elements of the language; but the very simplicity of the tasks they perform means that little or no thought needs to be devoted to the way in which the task is carried out. In the later stages of such a course the methods by which the tasks are to be carried out become more important; it becomes necessary to work out exactly how the task can be performed before one can express this in the language: it becomes necessary to formulate an *algorithm*.

In simple terms, an *algorithm* is set of instructions which describes how some task may be performed. Originally, the term was reserved for purely numerical processes, but in the context of computer programming it has acquired a wider meaning.

Examples of algorithms in this wider sense occur in everyday life: a recipe may be thought of as an algorithm describing the preparation of food, a knitting pattern as an algorithm to produce some garment. Computer programs are algorithms, in this case expressed in the rather specialized medium of a programming language. For the present, however, the fact that a computer program is an algorithm is purely incidental, since this section is concerned with the properties of algorithms that are apparent before they become computer programs.

This section is not intended as an algorithm designer's cook-book; rather, it will describe the properties that are shared by all algorithms, thus providing a basis for the analysis of existing algorithms and the design of new ones. Analysis and design are interdependent processes, in that it is not possible to be proficient at one without being proficient at the other.

Indeed, the final form of a design is arrived at only via many intermediate stages, at each of which analysis is carried out of the result so far, with a view to improving it.

An example of a simple algorithm is given below, which will be used to illustrate various points in the subsections that follow; we shall refer to it as 'the multiplication algorithm'.

Step 1 Put I equal to 0
2 Put P equal to 0
3 If N equals 0 or A equals 0 goto Step 7
4 Put P equal to P plus A
5 Put I equal to I plus 1
6 If I less than N goto Step 4
7 Put M equal to P
8 Stop

This algorithm defines the process of multiplication for positive integer values of N and A, giving the result in M. Like all algorithms, its purpose is to describe a task in terms of other tasks that have either been previously defined, or are considered sufficiently basic to be understood without definition.

Five crucial properties of algorithms

We shall discuss five properities that may be attributed to algorithms. These are: the *input* to an algorithm, the *output* it yields, the *definiteness* of its steps, the *effectiveness* of its steps, and its *termination.*

Referring back to the multiplication algorithm, it is clear that if it is to be executed then A and N must refer to numerical values: these two values are the input to the algorithm. The value that is calculated, M, is the output that it yields. Any well designed algorithm will possess two clearly defined and distinct sets of entities, constituting the input and the output. The contents of these two sets are referred to variously as 'parameters' or 'arguments'; the term *parameter* is the one that will be used here, since it is used to describe an object which remains constant for a given application of the algorithm, but which may change over several distinct applications.

The initial phase in the design of an algorithm is to decide on the contents of the input and output parameter sets. The second phase is to form an intuitive idea of the relationship between these two sets. The final phase is to resolve this intuitive idea into a formal set of instructions that define the relationship; this formal set of instructions is the algorithm.

For the algorithm to be of any use, each of the instructions referred to above must satisfy two criteria: definiteness and effectiveness.

Definiteness is meant to imply that an instruction is precisely and un-ambiguously defined: no doubt must exist as to what the operations invoked by the instruction consist of. If algorithms are expressed in English, or for that matter any other natural language, the possibility of such doubt will exist.

Consider, for example, Step 3 of the multiplication algorithm. It is clear that if N is zero we should go to Step 7, and similarly if A is zero; but what if both N and A are zero? In formal logic the condition A or B is true if A is true, or if B is true, or both; but in English the word 'or' is sometimes meant to exclude the case when both are true. So, unless we previously agree on the meaning of 'or', Step 3 is not definite.

A good definition of **effectiveness** is given by Knuth in his book *The Art of Computer Programming* (Volume 1). He says that an instruction is effective if the operations it involves are of a sufficiently basic nature to be performed by a man with pencil and paper in a finite amount of time. The ease with which one may write down instructions that are not effective is illustrated by the following.

Put X equal to the largest real value less than 1.

This is impossible: whatever value is chosen for X, a larger one may always be generated by adding any digit to the decimal expansion of the value. Thus if we choose 0.999, then 0.9994 is larger and still less than one; this instruction is clearly not effective. (N. B. for non-mathematicians: even '0.9 recurring' will not do, because it can be shown to equal 1). What is often not realized, because of the aura of exactitude and determinacy which surrounds computers, is that it is just as easy to write down non-effective steps in a programming language as it is in English.

The criterion of effectiveness is meant to eliminate impossible instructions from algorithms; definiteness is meant to eliminate vague, or meaningless instructions.

Unlike the last two properties, **termination** is a property of the algorithm as a whole rather than of the individual instructions. A simple example of an algorithm that does not terminate is the following:

> Step 1 Put I equal 1
>   2 Put I equal to $I+1$
>   3 Goto Step 2

Notice that this algorithm has empty input and output parameter sets, but this has not been specifically forbidden; notice also that the steps are both effective and definite, so, by the criteria established earlier it is a perfectly reasonable algorithm. However, once execution of the algorithm has begun there is no way in which it can come to an end: this algorithm does not terminate. That a particular algorithm does terminate is really something that needs proof, and even an informal proof is better than none. Such a proof for the termination of the multiplication algorithm might be: N represents a fixed, finite quantity; I represents a steadily increasing quantity, and the amount of the increase is constant; thus I cannot always remain less than N; therefore we shall not always return to Step 4.

Proof of termination is seldom as simple as this. However, it is possible to distinguish two broad classes of algorithm that require very different proof techniques.

Firstly, there are iterative numerical processes which yield approximate answers; termination of these normally involves obtaining an estimate of the error in the value obtained so far, and then comparing this with a predetermined accuracy criterion. Proof of termination in these cases would mean demonstrating that this criterion can be met, and this would normally involve mathematical analysis of the process in question. In fact, many of these processes have been extensively analysed, and the conditions under which they will terminate are well known and documented, but for some, no general proofs of termination are possible. This does not mean that these processes should not be used – they may be the only available methods – but it is as well to be aware of the problems that can arise when using them.

In connection with this class of algorithms, there is one very common source of error which may prevent proper termination even when the method is theoretically sound; this is rounding error. Rounding error is caused by the fact that real numbers are only stored approximately on a computer, and thus any algorithm that manipulates real quantities is prone to this source of error. As an example of the way in which rounding error occurs, consider a computer which stores real numbers with only two significant digits. Such a computer would represent the fraction 1/3 as .33. Now suppose that we try to multiply this fraction by 10, firstly by a straight multiplication, yielding the answer 3.3, and secondly by nine successive additions, which would yield, in sequence, 0.66, 0.99, 1.3 (at this stage we lose the third digit because our computer can retain only two digits) 1.6, 1.9, 2.2, 2.5, 2.8, 3.1. In terms of pure mathematics, which assumes total precision, both methods yield the same answer, but because of the rounding errors involved in a computing algorithm the addition method produces a less accurate answer than is obtainable by multiplication. It is the job of the algorithm designer to ensure that the method he uses takes account of the accuracy with which real numbers are stored, if this is relevant, or, preferably, to evolve a method that will always yield an answer which is as accurate as the machine makes possible. Actual computers, of course, work to greater precision than two significant figures, but this does not affect the principle.

The second class of algorithms is typified by non-numerical processes. For these a general proof of termination is usually possible, but often, more important questions are how soon they terminate, and how many steps are necessary to complete the process.

Sorting data into ascending order is one of the most thoroughly researched tasks of this second type. During the course of this research a great many different sorting algorithms have been developed, and for each method a proof of termination should – and for most of them does – exist, but the main thrust of the research has been towards finding out how quickly the task can be achieved for a given amount of data. This is not an easy question to answer, since with some sorting algorithms the time taken depends on the character of the data, for example whether it has any initial ordering.

Flow

The previous subsection dealt with what may be called the 'static' properties of algorithms; indeed, it could be said that it is an important part of the design of an algorithm to ensure that these properties are static throughout the execution of the algorithm. In contrast, this subsection will be devoted to the dynamics of algorithms: that is, those properties that change during execution.

Execution of an algorithm consists of proceeding from one step to the next, obeying the instructions of which each consists. However, every so often an instruction will be encountered that interrupts this well-disciplined and orderly flow. In the multiplication algorithm, Step 6 contains the instruction 'goto Step 4' which, provided that I is less than N, causes just such an interruption. The important aspects of this instruction are: (1) that it interrupts the normal flow from one step to the next; and (2) that it does this only when a certain condition is true. It is this second aspect that is crucial, for it is this conditional execution of an instruction that gives the algorithm its ability to change its behaviour during execution.

One very useful way of displaying the dynamic behaviour of an algorithm is that in which each instruction is represented as a point on a line; execution of the algorithm may then be seen as a flow along this line during which each instruction is obeyed as it is encountered. The advantage of this representation is that it shows, at a glance, all possible paths that may be taken during execution. The flow diagrams that are used by many programmers as a means of expressing algorithms are merely a more detailed form of this representation. Flow charting in relation to programming is discussed in Section 5.1.

Fig. 1.3A shows the multiplication algorithm in this form. This algorithm contains examples of the three types of flow that can occur: sequential, looping, and branching. These three types of flow are sufficient to describe all but a very special class of algorithms, namely those which include what is termed 'parallel execution'. This will be described later, but first let us examine the three basic types.

Sequential flow is used to describe the form of execution in which the steps of an algorithm are carried out in the order in which they are written. Steps 1, 2, 3 of the multiplication algorithm are an example of sequential flow.

Looping flow occurs when a set of steps is executed repeatedly: Steps 1, 5, and 6 are an example of this type of flow, and these steps are known collectively as a loop. This loop is executed a total of N times, and during each execution the steps it contains are executed sequentially; it should be understood that there is no contradiction here: whether we see the steps that comprise the loop as an example of sequential flow or of looping flow depends on whether we are considering just one execution of the loop, or its complete execution.

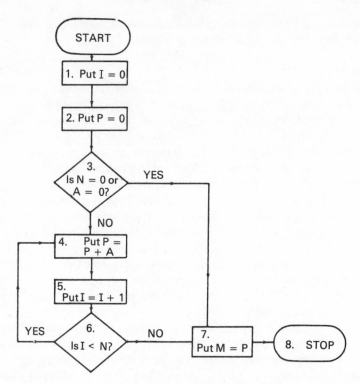

Fig. 1.3A – Flow chart of the multiplication algorithm.

Step 3 of the algorithm creates what is known as a **branch**: it provides for two alternative paths through the algorithm, the particular path taken being dependent on the values of N and A.

Before examining the general form of the branch it is worth comparing Steps 3 and 6, since they have very similar form and yet they define very different types of flow. Both steps involve the conditional execution of a goto statement: the condition of Step 3 is a little more complex than that of Step 6, but this is not an important difference from the present point of view. The essential difference between the two is that Step 6 can jump to a step that preceded it in the order of execution, whereas Step 3 cannot. Thus Step 6 has the potential to define a loop – and in this case it does – but Step 3 does not.

From now on we shall mean by 'branch' such a step which does *not* define a loop; one which does is included as part of the loop it defines. Note that branch steps do not, however, always point forward; it is possible to have backward branches which, because of the existence of further branches, do not define loops. Nevertheless, the similarity between Steps 3 and 6 in the example does demonstrate that flow is not something which can be determined by looking at individual steps; it can be deduced only from the algorithm as a whole. One advantage of the diagrammatic representation of an algorithm is that, *provided that it does not contain many steps,* a well-drawn diagram will reveal at a glance the types of flow it contains. The question which immediately follows is, how can one represent algorithms which do have many steps? The answer may be unexpected: *algorithms should never contain many steps,* and so the question should not arise!

Given that algorithms *in general* and *computer algorithms* in particular, are needed to solve very complex problems, this may seem an unachievable or even irrational objective. The resolution of the apparent inconsistency is simply that, if a task is so long and complicated that a single algorithm would be large and complex, it should always be split into smaller and simpler sub-tasks, for which algorithms should be designed individually. In fact, the first division into sub-tasks should be such that the structure of the overall algorithm and the flow between the sub-tasks is kept simple; if, as is likely, some of the sub-tasks are still large and complex, these in turn should be broken down, the process continuing in a *hierarchical* manner until all the sub-tasks at the lowest level have simple algorithms.

All this will be discussed again, in a more specifically computer context, in Sections 2.4 and 3.1. In fact, we can slightly ease the requirement that an algorithm should have a small number of steps, because it is the presence of branches which causes the real problem, and it is the number of those which should be kept as small as possible. Algorithms which contain only sequential and looping flow have a reasonably simple structure, and in general can contain more steps than those with branches, without causing difficulties, though the total number should still not be so many that the overall cumulative effect is unclear.

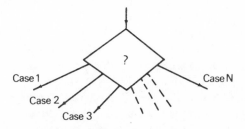

Fig. 1.3B — Multiple branching.

The general form of the branch is shown in Fig. 1.3B, that of Step 3 in the example being merely the simplest case. Every branch increases the number of alternative paths through the algorithm, and it is this property of the branch which causes the problem. There is no doubt that branches are necessary; but the more there are in an algorithm, the more complicated it becomes and the more difficult it is to understand what it is doing, or what path will be followed

in any particular circumstances. The consequences of this for program verification and testing are discussed in Section 3.1, while those for the readability
of program text are discussed in Section 2.4.

One consequence of the hierarchical method of algorithmic design (which
becomes 'structured programming' at the program writing stage) is that flow
charts for each sub-task and at each level of the hierarchy are reasonable simple
— so simple, indeed, that there are many who regard them as pointless, preferring
to express algorithms directly in some suitable language, typically a programming
language with good facilities for expressing loops of various kinds. In fact, the
expression of such simple algorithms should be reasonably simple whether one
uses flow charts, a suitable programming language, or even (provided that care is
taken over possibly ambiguity, as mentioned earlier) natural language. It is
largely a matter of taste how you do it; there are also many people who like the
visual reinforcement of the flow that the diagrammatic form gives, and certainly
it is a useful part of documentation, as mentioned in Section 5.1. If a flow chart
aids your understanding when designing an algorithm, fine; if it does not, there is
no point in using one — unless you need it to help discuss the algorithm with
someone else.

Parallelism and simultaneity

In the introduction to this section an algorithm was defined as a 'set' rather
than as a 'sequence' of instructions, the difference between the two terms being
that the latter implies some ordering of the instructions, whereas the former
does not. However, the algorithms we have met so far have all been ordered in
some sense: for example, the steps have been numbered, and we have referred to
a 'normal' sequence of execution which accords with this numbering. Therefore
the question now arises as to whether the word 'set' was necessary? Are there
algorithms in which the steps are not executed in a specific order? The answers
to both these questions is, yes!

Looking back at the multiplication algorithm, it should be clear that Steps 1
and 2 could be interchanged without affecting the outcome of the algorithm; the
same is true of Steps 4 and 5. Indeed, there is no reason why Steps 1 and 2 should
not be executed simultaneously; that is, in parallel. Computers that are capable
of parallel execution are so far relatively few, but there is little doubt that they
will become increasingly common. You may therefore at some time, if not
immediately, be faced with the necessity of designing algorithms to run on such
machines, and therefore having to recognize which steps can be carried out in
parallel and to use some notation for indicating this. For an informal description
of an algorithm, a reasonable notation would be one similar to that in Algol 68,
whereby instructions which can be executed in any order, and in particular in
parallel, are enclosed in brackets and separated from each other by commas.
To represent this form of execution diagramatically, a set of instructions enclosed
in brackets is represented by one point on a line (one box in a flow chart) since,

from the point of view of flow, it does not matter whether each point consists of one, or many, instructions, provided that such a set is genuinely independent of the order of execution.

The idea of parallel processing, as it is known, is a relatively new one, but it is one that will become of immense importance, especially to those that have to design algorithms, since they will have to evolve methods of using parallel processors efficiently. We shall return to this point briefly in Section 3.3.

Efficiency, Generality, Elegance

Given two different algorithms that perform the same task, it is likely that one of them will be judged to be better than the other. In this subsection we shall introduce three criteria that may form the basis for such judgements: algorithm X may be regarded as better than algorithm Y because it is more efficient, or because it is more general, or because it is more elegant.

Such a judgement is expressed in relative terms, and certainly in the case of **efficiency** it is usually difficult if not impossible to say that a given algorithm is 'efficient' in any absolute sense. Rather, the judgement is expressed relative to another algorithm, as above, or in relation to particular resources (such as execution time or storage requirements) or a particular kind of data (for example, one sorting algorithm can be regarded as efficient when working on very disordered data, but not on data which is fairly well ordered already, in which case a different algorithm may be preferred). This relativity, and the variety of criteria to relate to, can make judgement of efficiency very difficult. For example, it is well-known that often one can change an algorithm into a slightly different one which will run faster on a computer but will need more store — the 'time-store trade-off'; in what sense is this 'faster' algorithm more efficient than the other, especially if the larger store requirement means that the run receives lower priority in some scheduling algorithm in the operating system?

Given a definite criterion of efficiency to relate to, there are two main ways in which it might be possible to move from a given algorithm to a better one. The first is to retain the basic idea of the algorithm but to try to extract the

---

Algorithm A:
1 Put $X = 0$
2 Put $S = 0$
3 Put $I = I+1$
4 Put $S = S+I$
5 If $I<N$ goto Step 3

Algorithm B:
1 Put $S = N* (N+1)/2$

Fig. 1.3C — Algorithms for summing the first N natural numbers.

best out of it by adjusting its details or improving the way it is implemented. This is discussed in relation to the main machine resources of time and space in Section 3.3, and will not be pursued here. The second is to find a completely different algorithm. As a simple illustration, consider the two algorithms given in Fig. 1.3C for summing the first N natural numbers (the natural numbers are the ordinary counting numbers: 0, 1, 2, 3, 4. . .).

In algorithm A, as the value of N increases, the iterative process will take longer and longer; in algorithm B the process takes the same time for any N, subject only to large numbers taking a little longer to handle (for humans, not for machines within their normal range of operation!). Algorithm B is obviously more efficient except perhaps for very small N, and indeed in this case one can say it is efficient in an absolute sense. However, an algorithm designer who did not know the mathematical formula might never find it. A slightly less trivial case is the use of a computer algorithm to perform a numerical integration of some function, which a mathematician would be able to integrate analytically and obtain a formula to give the desired result directly.

These examples indicate that you should never simply use the first algorithm which comes to mind, without looking for alternatives; and that the best (known) algorithms for a given task often require specialist knowledge of the area of application. This of course reiterates what was said in the last section about the need to make thorough use of the literature.

The second criterion is that of **generality**, that is, the ability of an algorithm to cope with a wide class of problems rather than with a more limited class. An algorithm is normally designed originally to carry out one specific task, but it is often possible to see this task as a particular example of some more general process. One obvious advantage of this is that the algorithm will have a wider range of application, but there are others: design of the more general algorithm will usually give a greater insight into the problem; and by concentrating on similarities rather than differences, it may be possible to solve a whole range of problems which at first sight seem unrelated.

The process of generalizing an algorithm can often be achieved by an almost trivial change: the substitution of a variable for a constant is often all that is required. Consider, for example, the task of counting the words on this page of text. The nucleus of an algorithm for performing this task (though on its own it would not cope with all cases) would consist of incrementing a counter each time the character 'space' is encountered. By turning the character which causes incrementation into an input parameter, and invoking the algorithm with this parameter as a 'full stop', it could instead be made to count sentences. The particular task of counting words is now seen as an example of the more general problem of searching for 'delimiters' (spaces, full stops, commas) and taking some appropriate action when they are found.

The lessons to be learnt from the above example is that the method used to achieve a particular task often points the way to the method of generalization.

Above, the task of counting words was achieved by recognizing that each word is separated from the next by a space; from here it is a relatively easy step to seeing that each sentence is separated from the next by its own special character: a full stop.

In the above discussion various complications that can arise have been ignored, such as the problems created by multiple spaces at the end of a paragraph (which would be easy to get around), and the problem of abbreviations terminated by full stops (which would be harder to deal with). It is quite possible that the number of special cases that are generated by trying to generalize a given process will render the generalization useless, but then again one will at least have learnt something by trying.

This leads to the final point about the generality criterion: on occasion it will be in conflict with the efficiency criterion, in that a specific algorithm geared to a particular task may be able to take advantage of special features of that task which may not occur in the more general case.

The third criterion, that of elegance, is highly subjective and may be thought to be out of place in the present discussion. However, the term is quite commonly used by programmers when discussing the virtues of algorithms, and for that reason if for no other is worth some attention.

An **elegant** solution to a problem is one that is both simple and ingenious. Simple solutions are always to be commended, but whether ingenious solutions are equally desirable is open to question. The fact that a solution is described as ingenious implies that it is not obvious (which is considered by some to be a virtue, but, in itself, is not). The sort of problem that can arise is shown by the following algorithm:

1 Put $A=A+B$
2 Put $B=A-B$
3 Put $A=A-B$

This kind of trick, whose virtue is to interchange two values without the need for an intermediate copy of one of the values, is used by systems programmers in the context where, when exchanging the contents of registers, the saving of an extra register is important. Ingenious, certainly; elegant, perhaps, regarded as a particular rather than general solution taking into account the nature of the specific problem; but it is certainly inefficient when taken out of this context and used, say, to interchange two values of a multidimensional array in an ordinary program, and is also subject to rounding error if A and B are 'real number' values. Computer programming, perhaps more than any other field, abounds with so-called 'tricks of the trade'; many of these are necessary, but where they are used purely to demonstrate the mental agility of the programmer they are not, and they should thus be avoided.

Recursion

One very elegant general technique which deserves a subsection to itself is that of recursion. Recursion was developed as a means of defining functions by early research workers into the foundations of mathematics, and was later used by mathematical logicians. Because of the intimate relationship between their studies and the theoretical basis of computing, it has become an important topic.

From the present point of view recursion is of importance because it provides an elegant and very concise method of expressing algorithms. **Recursive** definitions, whether they be of functions or of algorithms, are characterized by the fact that the object being defined occurs in the definition itself. As an illustration, consider the following definition of the first N natural numbers:

Denoting the sum of the first N numbers by $S(N)$ we have:
$$S(N) = S(N-1)+N \quad (1)$$
$$S(1) = 1 \quad\quad\quad (2)$$

or in words: 'the sum of the first N numbers equals N plus the sum of the first $N-1$ numbers; and the sum of the first number is 1'.

In general, a recursive definition consists of two parts: one which relates the function evaluated at N to the function evaluated at $N-1$, and one which gives explicitly the function value for a constant value of the argument. As an illustration, consider the value of $S(5)$:

$S(5)=5+S(4)$ putting $N=5$ in (1) above; now, applying (1)
      with $N=4$ we obtain:
$S(4)=4+S(3)$ and after two more applications of (1) and one of (2),
      we have:
$S(5)=5+S(4)=5+4+S(3)=5+4+3+S(2)=5+4+3+2+S(1)=5+4+3+2+1$

There can be little doubt that the equations (1) and (2) given above constitute an algorithm for calculating the sum of the first N numbers; the question is, rather, whether it is a good algorithm for this task? Judged by most of the criteria set out earlier it is beyond reproach: it has a well defined input and output, its steps are effective and definite, and its termination has been demonstrated; it is certainly elegant, and it is completely general (given that N is constrained to be a positive integer). The only ground upon which it can be criticized is that of efficiency. On the other hand, a recursive algorithm can often be very easy to translate into a programming language which permits recursive definitions, which may lead to greater efficiency in implementation if not execution. The above algorithm translates into Algol 68 as

proc *sum* = (**int** *n*)**int**: **if** $n = 1$ **then** 1 **else** $n + sum(n-1)$**fi**

and such virtually direct transliteration is not uncommon. In this case non-recursive algorithms are easy too, but this is not true in other instances.

Another answer to the efficiency criticism is that where a program is to be run once only the cost incurred by the inefficiency of recursion may be offset by the cost of the extra testing runs required by a more complex, non-recursive version of the algorithm.

Recursion as a method of definition is not limited to numerical functions; indeed, it finds its most important range of applications in such areas as compiler writing, symbol manipulation, and combinatorial mathematics. The expressive power of a recursive definition is quite remarkable; in fact, it has been shown that functions exist which cannot be defined by the use of the ordinary arithmetic operations of $+$, $-$, $\times$ and $/$ between ordinary variables except by the use of recursion. Such a function is **Péter's function** defined below:

$$P(m+1,n+1) = P(m+1,n)$$
$$P(m+1,0) = P(m,1)$$
$$P(0,n) = n+1$$

This function, which is often referred to as **Ackermann's function**, provides an example of an algorithm whose termination for all positive integral values of m and n can be proved, but its value increases in magnitude so fast that it cannot reasonably be evaluated even for small values of its arguments m and n; to convince yourself of this try it for $P(4,4)$. It is worth pointing out that a language like Fortran that does not allow recursion is not, in any sense, less powerful than languages that do; the reason for this is that recursion can be 'mimicked' by using subscripted variables.

Where it arises naturally, recursion is an excellent method of expressing algorithms; its major disadvantage is that it tends to be inefficient in machine terms when executed. It has been argued that this is a result of the way that compilers are written rather than of the method itself, but however valid this may be it will not help the program to run any faster! The time and space efficiency of recursion is discussed further in Section 3.3. From the point of view of algorithmic design, if a recursive algorithm can easily be redefined in a non-recursive way, for example by a normal iterative process, then the non-recursive form should be used. However, if a non-recursive version is difficult to find, or is very complicated, it may, overall, be better to stick with the recursive one, paying something in final execution efficiency for increased understandability, reduced chance of error, and easier development.

Some practical implications

In this section we have outlined various properties and attributes that a well defined algorithm should have. The ideas discussed can be used not only as the basis for design, but as criteria for selecting an already existing algorithm. Here we summarize some of the practical implications of the earlier material.

The most important feature of any algorithm is what it does: what it requires as input, what it delivers as output, and how it transforms the input into the output.

There is also the question of correctness: does a proof of correctness exist? If not, is it possible to provide one?

If the algorithm terminates, is it certain to have produced the right answer? For a numerical algorithm one must ask, is the process vulnerable to rounding errors? Should the criterion for termination be relative or absolute? An absolute criterion implies that if the exact solution is x, then the algorithm will terminate as soon as the result r satisfies

$$x - \epsilon \leqslant r \leqslant x + \epsilon$$

where ϵ is the absolute error that can be tolerated. A relative error criterion would imply termination when r satisfies

$$x(1 - \epsilon') \leqslant r \leqslant x(1 - \epsilon')$$

where ϵ' is the proportionate error that can be tolerated. For any algorithm, non-numerical or numerical, one must consider how well it will cope with unexpected input data — for example, a systems programmer at a batch install-ation must have to take into account the possibility of a card deck being input upside down. All algorithms, indeed, should be resilient enough to stand up to unexpected input.

Finally, before any algorithm is translated into a programming language the designer should have some idea of the total number of steps involved in its execution with a given amount of data, so that some estimate of the amount of execution time can be made. A useful way of specifying this is to give the 'order' of the process: for example, the multiplication of two $n \times n$ matrics is an order n^3 process; that is, the number of steps, and thus the execution time, vary as the cube of n. Similarly, sorting n items of data by some methods is an order n^2 operation, but with the treesort algorithm it is of order $n \log n$. The documentation for any algorithm should always include an estimation of its order.

Paul Hide

CHAPTER 2

Program Writing

We now turn to the task of actually writing programs. The first section deals with the question of which language to use, and the second with the related matter of programming language standards, an important factor if the program is likely to be run under a variety of implementations. Section 2.3 discusses the choice of input and output media, something which often causes a good deal of trouble. Finally, in Section 2.4, the techniques of program writing which have become known as 'structured programming' are introduced, in a language-independent way, though illustrations using well-known languages are included.

2.1 CHOOSING THE LANGUAGE

Discussing the choice of programming language to use presupposes that a choice in fact exists. In many cases, a choice will not exist: whether through direction from above or through simple unavailability, it may be that no alternative will be provided to one specified language. In such situations the advice in this section will have no direct relevance. Nevertheless, the discussion which follows on choice of languages should still be of interest; and in that it involves assessing the merits of languages for dealing with particular problems, it will give some guidance on how to estimate how difficult a programming task will be when the language to be used is predetermined.

Beginners sometimes wonder why there are so many programming languages. Usually they have been introduced to programming with just one language, which has either been 'sold' to them by the person responsible for the introduction as being the 'best' language or at least the best available (in their opinion, that is); or which has simply been presented as it stands without reference to its merits or demerits or to the existence of alternatives, so the beginner just accepts it uncritically. Later, when other languages are brought to their attention, people taught in this way (though 'introduced' is a better term, since 'taught' can be an overstatement) often tend to think of other languages as a (probably tiresome) irrelevance. This may be because 'their' language is perfectly all right thank you, or because surely one language is much the same as another, or because all languages have their good points and bad points, their supporters and their detractors, and how can one possibly decide between them; in all of which cases, is it not simpler just to stick with the one that you know?

It is essential for anyone who is going to write programs seriously, either as a professional programmer or in the course of other work, to recognize three things. One is that programming languages do vary in quality, and that some are better than others according to given criteria. Another is that even the best languages (according to such criteria) are not perfect, and there will be circumstances in which they will be less than ideal, and indeed inferior to other languages. The third is that even generally poor languages (according to such criteria) usually have strengths as well as weaknesses, so that such a language may validly be found preferable in some situation to a generally better language, if the nature of the problem happens to require its particular strengths. In consequence, a truly professional programmer, or a fully competent amateur programmer, will be prepared to tackle problems in a range of languages, to find the best (or best available) for a given problem. He may even go to the lengths of learning a new language for the purpose rather than forcing the problem, or its solution, into a mould required by a language which is less suitable. Most of the rest of this section gives some guidelines about what to look for. No attempt will be made to discuss comprehensively the strengths and weaknesses of particular existing languages, though some examples will be given as illustrations.

Opinions differ so much about programming languages and their relative merits because there are many valid criteria for judging them. Many different ways legitimately exist for giving relative weights and priorities to these various criteria, and indeed between some there can be at least potential and sometimes actual conflict: for example, between readability and conciseness, or between efficiency and security. The important thing for the programmer to do is, firstly, to be consciously aware of these criteria and to apply them rationally and dispassionately, and, secondly, to relate them, and the relative weights to be attached to them, to the needs of the particular problem in hand. As far as possible he should try to be aware of, and make conscious allowance for, his own particular preferences, both for languages and for criteria; programmers are as prone to rationalization of instinct and *a posteriori* argument as anyone else. Whether your natural inclination is towards achieving maximum run-time efficiency or maximum readability or maximum security, there will be occasions on which these favourite criteria will be of less significance than others, or at least where the price to be paid for the maximum is too great.

Closely related to the question of criteria for judging languages is that of criteria for *designing* languages. Awareness of the design aims of various languages will give some guidance as to their suitability for different applications, though of course languages vary in the amount of success which was achieved in meeting the design aims. The age of the language is relevant here; broadly speaking, the older the language the less clearly defined the design aims are likely to be, in the sense that in addition to the explicit aims, some would have been taken for granted, whereas other possible criteria might not have been given much consideration at all. Thus Fortran, designed for ease of expression of scientific formulae, comes from a time when it was taken for granted that maximizing run-time efficiency was of overriding importance, because then processor time was at a premium. Nowadays many languages are as good as or better than Fortran in expressing scientific formulae, and, more generally, handling scientific problems, so if that is the dominant criterion there are better choices. Nevertheless run-time efficiency is still an important consideration, if nowadays less overriding, and scientific programs are still being written which stretch today's most powerful machines to their limits, so it is this characteristic of Fortran rather than its original explicit design aim which remains one of its main strengths *vis-a-vis* other languages. On the other hand, criteria such as security and the provision of good control structures and facilities hardly entered into consideration at all in the design of Fortran, while standards in areas such as readability of program text have become much higher since it first appeared.

The essence of the art of choosing a language is to start with the problem, decide what its requirements are, and their relative importance, since it will probably be impossible to satisfy them all equally well. The available languages should then be measured against the list of requirements, and the most suitable (or least unsatisfactory) chosen. Some criteria will relate to the applications area and the nature of the algorithmic processes and computations involved. Some will relate to the environment in which the program is to run, its likely mode of use, the peripherals it needs, etc. Some will relate to purely logistic considerations such as the timescale and facilities allowed for development, questions of convenience, acceptability of the choice to others, and so on. Conditions can vary so wildly that there is no point in trying to suggest how one determines the relative importance of these considerations other than by treating each case on its merits, except to note that considerations of short-term convenience are, humans being what they are, commonly allowed too much weight.

Considering first of all criteria which relate to the problem itself, an important factor is the kind of processing which will be involved. It is commonplace to talk of the distinction between 'scientific' and 'commercial' processing as if this was the only difference that mattered. In the early days of computers it probably was, and of course it is still important, but the reality now is much more complicated. Many scientific problems show features usually characterized as 'commercial'; a smaller but still significant proportion of commercial problems require 'scientific' facilities; and some problems do not fall easily into either category. Further, there are wide variations even within each broad area. It is more sensible to consider what the various requirements are for different kinds of processing, for the given problem.

One criterion is the kind of *arithmetic* involved. A problem may require any or all of integer, fixed-point, floating-point, or complex number arithmetic. In any of these categories the required precision and range of calculation must be taken into account. If detailed control over these factors is needed, a language like PL/I may be the most suitable; more likely, it is just that the problem requires sufficient precision and sufficient range to be available for its solution, in which case the choice is wider and is implementation-dependent. For example, a problem which on one machine might need Fortran DOUBLE PRECISION or Algol 68 **long real**, might not on a machine with longer word length, in which case languages without built-in double-length arithmetic would be equally suitable in this respect.

The next criterion concerns the kind of *data structures* involved in the problem. Most languages provide facilities for arrays, so if this is the most complicated data structure needed, the choice is wide, though there are variations between languages over matters like number of dimensions allowed, permitted range of subscripts, and built-in facilities for array handling which may be important in particular cases. If more flexible data structures are needed, then languages like Cobol, Pascal, PL/I or Algol 68 will be more suitable in this respect than ones like Fortran, Algol 60, or Basic. Where the flexibility is very great, list-processing and similar languages, like Lisp, should be considered.

Next comes the question of the *complexity* of the problem, in terms of the amount of decision-taking, looping etc. involved, and how interconnected this is. If this is very limited, then languages with poor control facilities like Basic or Fortran may nevertheless be adequate; if it is very great, then languages like Algol 68 and Pascal with very good control facilities will score, and use of languages which are weaker in this respect will probably have to be paid for in terms of increased time and difficulty in development, and loss of security.

Another criterion is the amount of *text-handling* or similar non-numerical computation involved. Languages like PL/I, Algol 68, and Fortran 77 have facilities of varying degrees of sophistication for handling character strings, but special-purpose languages such as Snobol, designed for such applications, are also worth serious consideration.

Another important application area for which special-purpose languages have been designed is *real-time processing* such as the monitoring and/or control of industrial or laboratory processes. If facilities are needed for this, then such languages as Coral 66 or RTL/2 must clearly be considered, as well as general-purpose languages with suitable facilities (for example Algol 68 and PL/I again, and concurrent Pascal). If none of these is available it may be necessary to fall back on real-time extensions to languages such as Basic and Fortran, if these can be found, or ultimately to assembly-language, whether in modules embedded in other languages, or for the complete program. Real-time processing and its special problems are discussed further in Section 4.5.

Finally, there is the criterion of what need exists for extensive *file-handling*. Especially if the program is to be transportable, the use of languages with facilities built-in, such as Cobol, should be considered; in languages without them it is then necessary to use operating system facilities directly in job control language, which is inevitably much more implementation-specific.

The next batch of criteria concern the environment in which the program is to be used, and its mode of use, in particular whether it is to be a *batch* or an *interactive* program. If the program is designed to be run interactively, the choice may be between languages designed specifically for such use, such as Basic or APL, and adaptations, usually very system-dependent, of batch languages such as Fortran. The success of such adaptations does vary, and in general the specially designed languages may be safer bets in this respect; however, in other respects they may be lacking, especially in particular facilities needed.

Under this general heading come questions of *efficiency* and *size,* both of the compiler and of the compiled code; both are obviously very implementation-dependent, but there may be limitations either of the machine itself, or imposed by budgetary or allocation restraints, or of guaranteed turnround, which will preclude otherwise suitable languages in particular cases, or at least render them less attractive. Another factor is the support given to *special machine facilities* which you may need to use, such as a graph plotter or microfilm; it may be that access to these facilities can only be made, or only conveniently be made, with certain languages.

Similar considerations arise for purely logistic reasons, which form the last batch of criteria. These concern matters like *convenience of use* and *timescale for development,* where, for example, it may be sensible to make use of a given applications package in an otherwise less suitable language, rather than have to write your own equivalent in a more suitable language. *Facilities for development* must also be taken into account, including such matters as whether there is interactive or fast batch turnround available in a given language, the quality of the compiler diagnostics, the availability of adequate documentation and support. *Transferability* of the finished program may also be a factor, as may *maintainability,* which bring in questions of whether the language is standardized (formally or *de facto*), ease of writing readable and secure code, the acceptability of the chosen language to potential recipients, future persons responsible for its maintenance, and so on. There is a great deal of difference, as will be seen again later, between writing a quick one-off program which will be discarded once the results have been obtained, and something which is going to be a production program for a period of years. The only point to add here is that it quite often turns out that the presumed 'one-off' program turns out to be needed again later.

By now, the potential for conflict between the various criteria which was mentioned earlier will be amply apparent. As indicated before, often there is no easy way of resolving such conflict in a particular instance, and certainly the different weights and priorities to be accorded to each vary greatly from problem to problem. It is often a relief if the decision is taken out of your hands, even if on no better grounds than 'we'll use Cobol because we always use Cobol', or 'we won't use Fortran because it's a rotten language' regardless of their suitability for the particular problem. But, if the decision is yours, assess the problem as well as you can, think of all the criteria which might possibly apply, and don't just accept the popular or fashionable images of the various available languages, but find out for yourself. You will then be in a good position to defend your decision if you have to; and at least you will have the satisfaction of knowing that you have made it to the best of your ability, on rational technical grounds, rather than through prejudice or inertia.

Brian Meek

2.2 PROGRAMMING LANGUAGE STANDARDS

In the last section the transferability of the finished program to other install-ations was mentioned as one possible criterion for choice of language. If trans-ferability is required merely to other machines of the same kind, presumably all languages available on your machine will be available on the others, and so the problem disappears, though there may be other problems of the kind discussed in Section 5.3. Where, however, the program is potentially transferable to computer sites with machines of many different ranges, the choice is effectively restricted to one of the generally available languages, including those like Fortran and Cobol which have been the subject of international standardization, and others which, though not formally standardized, have generally-recognized definitions. However, as this section will show, choice of one of these languages does not end the problems.

In the early days of computer languages a language was defined largely by its compiler, and when a point of difficulty arose that did not appear to be adequately covered by the available manual, the way to settle it was to try it on the machine. This approach leads to a number of difficulties, since a programmer may learn in detail just what can be expected on the only machine he uses, while remaining quite unaware that another model of computer, apparently using the same language, will behave quite differently. Furthermore, this approach makes it difficult to assign responsibility for the agreement of a compiler and its documentation; if a compiler and its manual disagree, is the manual wrong for failing to describe the compiler correctly or is the compiler wrong for failing to implement the language that the manual describes?

The Algol Report of 1960 was a considerable step forward in this respect, in defining a language in considerable detail, without reference to any particular machine, in a defining document that could be regarded as the arbiter in all cases of dispute. Some difficulties have arisen in the interpretation of this document, but in general it has stood the test of time remarkably well. It failed, however, to standardize on two important matters: (i) the hardware representation of the language; (ii) the instructions to be used for input and output operations. The differences between one Algol 60 compiler and another in these two matters are sufficiently glaring, that anyone who wishes to transfer a program from one machine to another cannot fail to be aware of these two hurdles; but once they have been overcome the rest of the transfer is easy, because both machines are likely to have stuck closely to the definition of the language.

Very different is the case with Fortran, which had existed in a number of versions for many years before any attempt was made to produce a standard definition. So many incompatibilities existed that the standard could not try to be more than a common subset, unless it were to support one manufacturer's implementation at the expense of invalidating another's.

Among subsequent languages, Cobol, PL/I, Algol 68, Pascal, and APL have followed the pattern of Algol 60 in being defined first and implemented later, while Basic is following the painful path of Fortran, attempts being made to reach a standard definition after many years of use in various implementations.

In the remainder of this section, we shall consider Fortran in some detail, as the problems are probably greatest there. It can in fact be said that the vast majority of Fortran programs are not in accordance with the standard, and that a large proportion of Fortran programmers are not aware of the limitations that the standard imposes.

Limitations of space preclude similar discussion of the other formally or informally standardized languages, but programmers must always be aware that, for reasons good or bad, any implementation of any standard language is likely to depart in some respect from the standard. Therefore, if there is any chance that a program will later be transferred to another machine, the programmer should make it his business to discover where the variations occur and to avoid the non-standard features if this is reasonably possible. The discussion of Fortran which follows highlights the kinds of problem which are caused if non-standard features are used, and will give some indications of the kind of thing to look out for. It will also offer some guidance on what to do if the 'cure' of avoiding a non-standard feature seems no better than the 'disease' of using it.

The Fortran standard in use at the time of writing (mid-1978) is the ANSI 1966 or ISO 1972 version (the two are virtually identical), and this version will be considered as 'the standard' for present purposes. The new version, Fortran 77, has been accepted by the standardizing authorities, but experience with Cobol suggests that pre-Fortran 77 versions will continue in use for some years after Fortran 77 compilers begin to appear, which at the time of writing has not yet occurred. It is therefore too early to predict what the effect of the new standard will be upon what programmers and installations actually do. For the time being, only the older standard can be considered as a practicable basis for transferability.

The 1966 standard being no more than a common subset, the question arises of whether good programming practice should seek to constrain itself within this subset, or whether it is reasonable to take advantage of the extra facilities that most Fortran compilers include, and that manufacturers advertise as being so desirable. Some of these extra facilities are in the form of language extensions, others of relaxation of restrictions. Many questions need to be asked to determine which, if any, of them should be used.

Sometimes you will find that a non-standard feature is compulsory. For example, on an ICL 1900 computer, the main program must start with a MASTER statement, and the final program unit must be terminated by a FINISH line following its END line. Either you use these features, or you cannot use Fortran on that machine at all. Similarly, it may sometimes be necessary to use a non-standard feature or forgo the use of part of the machine hardware. On a PDP-11, for example, the statement

$$\text{READ (15'10) M}$$

which is distinguished from a standard READ statement only by the apostrophe instead of a comma, will read into variable M the 10th item from a random-access disk file identified as unit 15. If you refuse to use this feature, you cannot access such a file. However, there is a great deal to be said in favour of restricting its use (and that of the corresponding WRITE statement) to within a single subroutine, through which all such accesses are made, rather than distributing it throughout the program. To change machines, only the one subroutine will then have to be changed — if this is the only problem.

There are other non-standard features whose use is a matter of convenience rather than of compulsion. For example, the standard is much more restrictive than most compilers in the types of integer expression that may be used in a subscript. Thus

$$\text{A(I + J) = B}$$

is illegal in the standard language. Instead you must use two statements such as

$$\text{IPLUSJ = I + J}$$
$$\text{A(IPLUSJ) = B}$$

This latter construction is clumsy in comparison. Is it really necessary to use it?

A purist might argue that although it is clumsy it is not difficult to do, and once one's guard is lowered it is very difficult to know where to stop. Counter-arguments would be that the first version is simpler to write, is a little more efficient on the machine, makes clear the exact intention (in the second version it is not clear whether the new value of IPLUSJ is being set for some additional purpose also), will work on almost every compiler and, above all, is *fail-safe*. That is to say, if it is allowed, the interpretation is so clear that there can be no doubt about its effect, while if it is not allowed it seems certain to produce an error message rather than the execution of unintended operations. One possible criterion to use when resolving such problems is that the new (Fortran 77) standard does permit such constructs. In otherwise similar situations where the new standard does not permit the construct, this fact may constitute an additional reason for avoiding it.

Even the purist, though, will wilt before some of the requirements of the standard. Thus the standard does not allow

```
DIMENSION P(5)
DATA P/5*0.0/
```

but insists on

```
DIMENSION P(5)
DATA P(1), P(2), P(3), P(4), P(5)/5*0.0/
```

and if the size of the array were 1000 instead of 5 this would be quite intolerable. Again, the first version is simpler, allowed by nearly all compilers, and fail-safe.

However, it is better to avoid such a construction as

```
DIMENSION P(5)
DATA P/3*0.0/
```

where the number of elements of the array is not the same as the number initialized, as some compilers will accept the partial initialization but others reject it; and it is extremely foolish to use

```
REAL A/3.0/
```

since it does nothing whatever that

```
DATA A/3.0/
```

would not have done, is rejected by many compilers, and is in neither the 1966 standard nor the later (Fortran 77) one.

To avoid such constructions, however, it is necessary that Fortran programmers should have a knowledge of what is allowed by the Fortran standard, and it appears that all too many of them do not.

Again, a construction in widespread use is

```
SUBROUTINE X(A, N)
DIMENSION A(1)
```

where the 1 is merely a dummy and, in effect, tells the compiler: 'You need to know that this is a one-dimensional array, but you do not need to know how long it is, so I shall not tell you'. If, as is often the case, the upper bound of the array is needed for other purposes and is therefore passed across as an argument, it might as well be used. Thus

```
SUBROUTINE X(A, N)
DIMENSION A(N)
```

brings it within the standard and is therefore preferable. However, if the size of the array is 2*N+1, for example, yet N is also needed, the requirements of the standard can be met only by means of an additional argument, for example

```
SUBROUTINE X(A, N, M)
DIMENSION A(M)
```

with a CALL statement such as

```
CALL X(A, N, 2*N + 1)
```

or by

```
SUBROUTINE X(A, M)
DIMENSION A(M)
N = (M - 1)/2
```

either of which some programmers would think unnecessarily fussy and in-efficient when the original version, using 1 as a dummy, works perfectly well.

In this context, Fortran 77 still disallows the dummy 1, but has the new construction DIMENSION A(*) instead. Unfortunately, however, this asterisk is not being allowed for an array as the last item of blank COMMON, where the dummy 1 can also be useful.

The non-standard constructions considered so far are fairly benign. The best advice is probably to keep within the restrictions of the standard so far as you *reasonably* can. In particular, the discipline of doing so, and the knowledge that it gives of the standard, means that you are much less likely to go astray in· those matters where it really is of importance not to do so. Three of the more difficult areas will now be discussed.

The first is character handling. Fortran is principally designed as a language for expressing mathematical operations, and the means whereby mathematical variables are allowed to contain representations of characters are a rather incon-sistent afterthought. To a large extent the 1966 standard is not so much restrict-ive as simply absent-minded concerning what, if anything, can be done with characters, but if taken literally it appears that to read them in and print them out is about the limit. In particular, it appears that, if J and K each contain characters, then both

```
N = J
```

and

```
IF (J .EQ. K) GO TO 10
```

are non-standard operations, and indeed both can fail on certain machines in some circumstances. Of course, this can be regarded as an instance of using a language unsuitable for the particular purpose (and Fortran 77, as well as many other languages, makes it much easier) but, as many have found, very often Fortran is the only language able to guarantee the maximum transportability (in other respects).

It would not be reasonable to recommend that such usage of characters must be avoided, since these operations are of the essence in some programs; but because of machine dependence they are best handled by special subprograms that can be adjusted for different machines. Thus the two statements above might become something like

```
CALL CHASS(N, J)
IF (EQUAL(J, K)) GO TO 10
```

(where the name CHASS is derived from CHaracter ASSignment, and EQUAL is a LOGICAL FUNCTION). It would also be valid to use

```
CALL CHASS(N, 1HA)
```

but not

```
IF (EQUAL(J, 1HA))
```

since a Hollerith constant may be used as an argument to a subroutine but not to a function — one of the totally inexplicable features of the 1966 Fortran standard that is actually enforced by some compilers.

A second place where non-standard operations can cause real trouble relates to the association of variables through argument lists. Consider the following:

```
      M = 12
      N = 18
      CALL A(M, N)
      WRITE (6,15) M
   15 FORMAT (1X,I7)
      STOP
      END
      SUBROUTINE A(J, K)
      J = 5
      WRITE (6,10) K
   10 FORMAT (1X,I7)
      RETURN
      END
```

Some compilers use internal variables within a subroutine to represent dummy arguments, and using a 'copy-in, copy-out' mechanism would execute the above program as

```
      M = 12
      N = 18
      J = M
      K = N
      J = 5
      WRITE (6,10) K
   10 FORMAT (1X,I7)
      M = J
      N = K
      WRITE (6,15) M
   15 FORMAT (1X,I7)
      STOP
```

Other compilers use an 'indirect addressing' mechanism for dummy arguments, and would execute it as

```
        M = 12
        N = 18
        M = 5
        WRITE (6,10) N
    10 FORMAT (1X,I7)
        WRITE (6,15) M
    15 FORMAT (1X,I7)
        STOP
```

The standard is carefully written so that either of these methods is valid, and will give the same results for standard-conforming programs; in either of the above implementations the numbers 18 and 5 will be printed, but if we change

```
        CALL A(M, N)
```

to the non-standard

```
        CALL A(M, M)
```

the first implementation will print 12 and 12, and the second will print 5 and 5.

This sort of trouble may occur not only when the same actual argument corresponds to more than one dummy argument, but also when an actual argument is held in common storage; the rules in the standard to prevent trouble are quite complicated to understand, to remember, and to ensure.

A third troublesome area concerns the execution of loops in non-standard conditions. The statement

```
        DO 50 J = 1, N
```

is illegal in the standard if N is less than 1. The majority of compilers will not detect a fault if N=0, but some will execute the body of the loop once, some zero times, and some twice (on the assumption that this is shorthand for 1,N,−1). Woe betide the programmer who uses such a construction, knowing well what it does, and then changes to another machine. Experience shows that the resulting 'bugs' can be most disturbing, particularly if the N=0 condition only rarely occurs, so that the program runs well nearly all the time.

This particular trouble shows well why it is not possible to design a compiler that will itself report at compile-time all things that are not in accordance with the standard. Some of them cannot be detected until run-time.

Non-standard constructions that will run on different machines with different effects are the ones that should be avoided at all costs.

If you submit an algorithm to a journal that publishes them, you may find that it is willing to accept anything that can be demonstrated to work on a particular machine. Thus one sometimes sees in journals notations that are well known to programmers for a particular range of computers but are quite unknown to other programmers or to the standard, such as REAL*8. Such algorithms are often relatively useless, as one of the objects of publication should be to present something that others can use as a 'black box', understanding the input required for it, and the output expected from it, without having to understand the internal workings.

Far more useful from this point of view are the algorithm publications in those journals whose editors insist on full adherence to standard languages, as these usually can be used in 'black-box' fashion with success. It may be annoying for an author to have his submission rejected for using features that are almost universally implemented, but no other policy will give the required assurance of algorithms that can be fully trusted by potential users. Holding a line at the level laid down by the standard is a clear policy that everyone can at least understand, and can check for themselves without having to refer to the journal for a ruling on whether a certain feature is to be allowed or not. There is no other place at which a similar stand can be made. Thus if you are writing for publication, the standard should be followed as rigorously as possible.

As mentioned earlier, while this section has dealt in detail with the problems in Fortran, the kinds of problem and the kinds of approach to use in deciding on a solution to them should give an indication of the things to look out for in other languages, and how to deal with the problems as they arise.

I. D. Hill

2.3 CHOICE OF INPUT-OUTPUT

An important aspect of program design is the input-output to be used. It is often overlooked because for beginners it tends to be very simple and laid down in advance, and their main problems are in controlling the formatting facilities in the language they are using. However, in many problems it does have to be considered with some care, especially when using big computer systems with a wide variety of facilities.

Considering output first, much depends on whether the program is batch or interactive, and we shall see this distinction appearing under various headings. Computer output can be broadly characterized into the categories of (a) text, (b) graphics, (c) machine-readable (usually text or binary), and (d) others for special purposes, for example for real-time control. For the moment we shall consider the problems involved in category (a), leaving discussion of the variations and special characteristics of the others until later.

The principal factors to be taken into account with textual output are its *volume* and its *permanence*. Clearly it is only high volume output which causes a problem, though it has to be remembered that this term is a relative one, dependent on the output device; what is low volume for a 1000 lines per minute line printer may be high volume for a 10 character per second teleprinter.

In most computer systems the normal batch output device is a line printer, and it is worth finding out what its speed is, and whether there are any system limitations on the number of lines allowed, or penalties (in terms of turnround or cost) for programs generating a large number of lines of output. A big system may have a choice of printers with different characteristics. Line width is also an important factor; in general it is good practice to attempt to use line width to the full, subject to the need to produce well laid out, readable output, and any additional constraints such as the need to be compatible with systems with narrower line widths. Where the device is a character-by-character printer rather than a line-by-line printer this is less important (except for paper-saving); it is the number of characters generated and the character per second speed which matter. With such devices it is worth while to find out if they have tabulator controls, and design layout of output text accordingly.

If the volume of output is high (for example, will run to several minutes on the particular device, or will cause some system limit to be violated) it is worth looking for alternatives. The first question to ask is, whether all that output is really needed. In general, programmers do tend to produce more output than they need. Admittedly this is a lesser fault than writing a program which will use several minutes of processing time and then get aborted without having generated any output at all; but often it is difficult to believe that an output of hundreds of lines is really going to be read. Possibilities are: to refine the definition of the problem so that the output expresses more concisely what is needed; to cut out intermediate output inserted at an earlier stage to aid development; to look at formats, for example of numerical output, to see if the precision or range provided for in the output is really justified; and to output only a selection or summary, accepting that on occasion a re-run producing more output may be needed.

This last possibility depends very much on the nature of the problem, and in this case, or when all the output is genuinely needed, for example for reference or archiving purposes, it may be desirable to combine summary or selected output with full output on some other medium. Suitable high volume media are microfilm (or microfiche), magnetic tape, and disk file. Choice among these will depend on availability, cost, and convenience, in particular on the permanence of the output, the other major factor. Most permanent are files for record or archiving purposes, or for indefinite future reference. If they are not to be machine readable then microfilm or microfiche is indicated if available. If it is not available and the output must be printed, it may be appropriate to output to tape or disk and do the printing either offline or as a low-priority job later. If the permanence is uncertain, a disk file which can be deleted if the selected printout indicates it is not needed, or copied if it is needed, is one appropriate solution. This also copes with the situation when output is ephemeral in the sense that it needs to be available for consultation for a limited period only, and then discarded; it can be kept on file and then either subjected to further selected copying (suitable, for example, for batch/magnetic tape) or to interactive access and scanning from a visual display terminal (suitable for disk). The same applies when the selected or summary printout for output which might be needed to be archived does not, for some reason, provide sufficient guidance. The aim throughout should be to confine the actual printed output to what is reasonably certain to be needed immediately, keeping the rest available until either it is needed, or it can be discarded, within the limitations of the facilities of the system used.

Much of this applies to interactive as well as batch systems, with the additional note that the default output device in an interactive system is the terminal itself. This is of lower capacity than a line printer, which therefore in its turn can be used to take output which would be too great in volume for a terminal. Any interactive program which produces high-volume output without the need for user intervention should be designed with this possibility in mind, assuming of course that a printer is available.

The other point to note with interactive systems is that terminals themselves vary in respect of speed and capacity. Printing terminals usually operate at between 10 and 30 characters per second, though faster ones do exist, for example matrix printers with keyboards; visual display terminals, however, commonly operate at 100 characters per second and above. Another point to note is that VDU output is ephemeral (unless captured by user action with a photographic or other hard-copy attachment) and so is unsuitable in general for output which will be needed for later reference. Also, the display capacity of such a terminal is limited, so this factor has to be borne in mind, plus points like whether the operating system automatically 'pages' output greater than this capacity, that is, pauses when the screen is full for the user to read and then signals for more output, or whether the programmer himself has to make allowance for it in the program.

In general, an interactive program will be slightly different for printing terminals and visual display terminals, the former producing less output at a time but exploiting the fact that the user can refer back easily to what he did earlier or what was output earlier, the latter allowing for the limited capacity of the display but exploiting its higher speed. When writing such a program, therefore, it is desirable to know the kinds of terminals which will be used, and to take their various limitations into account. One point often overlooked is that, while trailing blanks at the end of a line do not matter for a line printer, they do for an interactive terminal printing one character at a time. The same applies to output layouts where widely spaced columns are used, or text is offset to the right, unless the terminal has tabulating facilities which can be used to reduce the delay caused by the output of a long succession of blanks. Similar considerations apply to light-duty or low-cost printers on batch systems which are character rather than line printers, though the delays are there usually less irritating than to an interactive user.

Turning now to the question of graphics output, the same general considerations apply, except that the choice is usually more limited. At present the normal means of graphical output are microfilm, incremental plotter, graphics display, and simulation on some textual medium such as a line printer. Often one is lucky to have more than one of the first three available. Line printer simulation, popular for student exercises and for the surreptitious production of Snoopys or nudes, is suitable only for low volume and where low quality is acceptable, though still worth considering as a means of giving a rough indication of what a proper graphics device would produce. Better for this purpose, however, is output on a graphics terminal, especially if combined with an interactive editing facility to enable things like axes and scales to be adjusted before sending the data for plotting more permanently, or using a hard-copy attachment. The primary uses of a graphics terminal, however, are for applications like computer aided design, computer aided learning, real-time monitoring, and so on, in which case it chooses itself. As for the permanent media, microfilm is suitable for low or high volume, the digital plotter only for low volume but very valuable where large, accurate, high-quality hard copies are needed. Microfilm is usually generated offline from a magnetic tape; it is worth investigating with any form of graphical output whether this is possible, or to consider using intermediate output, say to a disk file, and generating the graphics with a separate, low-priority job, especially in the case of high volume.

Some machine-readable output media have already been mentioned. Magnetic tapes (of the standard half-inch variety) or exchangeable disk packs are suitable for high volume, cassette tapes or floppy disks (usually only available on small systems) for lower volume, permanently online disk files for low to medium volume especially where the information is in very frequent use or subject to frequent change. Media like punched cards or paper tape are really suitable only for low volume output. Some programmers have a habit of wanting large amounts of punched output, perhaps because they feel more comfortable with familiar things, or because they cannot be bothered to learn about alternatives, or because they are afraid that things will go wrong with magnetic media – for example, tapes will be corrupted or disk files will be lost. In this last case, such fears are sometimes not unfounded; however, it is necessary to consider the costs involved (direct costs of punching, and consequential costs of storage, subsequent input, etc). and general convenience, for example the risks of something going wrong if the magnetic media are used, the seriousness of the consequences if something does go wrong, and so on. One advantage of punched card or paper tape output (if it is not binary) is that it can be understood by humans, in particular for offline hand editing.

The final category of output was a general one covering all kinds of signals for the control of specific processes and equipment. The requirements can, indeed, be so specific that there is little point in devoting much space to them. Perhaps the major points to note are that it is possible that the programmer will need in such cases to learn more about the electronics of the signals than many find comfortable or appropriate; and that in any case much attention will have to be given to external time constraints, often far more complex and demanding than the mere concern with turnround or operating system time limits or inter-active response times which face programmers in conventional environments.

Some features discussed under output appear again when we turn to input. The questions of volume, and of the speeds of the various devices, are naturally again important. Nevertheless there are substantial differences; the apparent sym-metry in computing between input and output, often reflected in programming languages, is deceptive.

An important consideration is whether the input data is *captive,* that is, already recorded in some form, or whether data capture is part of the design problem. If data is captive, the next consideration is whether it is recorded in machine-readable form (for example a magnetic tape which has been written to by another program, or a cassette or paper tape produced by a data logger) or some other (usually manuscript or typescript) which will have to be transcribed into machine input by some means, in which case such transcription is part of the design problem.

Having the data captive in machine-readable form looks to be the simplest situation. In fact it can cause many more headaches than having to make decisions about data capture or transcription, the reasons being that (by a well-known law variously attributed to Finagle, Murphy, or less printable alternatives) commonly the form of the captured data is less than ideal for the purposes of the problem, or not wholly compatible with the computer system to be used, or both. Many computer departments or services have experienced the inward sinking feeling when a new customer comes in through the door carrying a magnetic tape and smiling broadly 'No problem, all the data's on here!', knowing that very likely he will have no idea of how the data is formatted, what recording density was used, what blocking and labelling conventions were used, possibly even what machine produced it or whether it is 7-track or 9-track. Even card codes, and to a lesser extent paper tape codes, can cause problems, and programmers faced with captive data in any medium will have to be prepared to face them, and to extract from the captive data the particular data he needs and to convert it into the form he wants. He may even find it worth while to separate out this problem from the main one, and write a program solely to input the captive data and output it, for example to disk or tape, in a form more suitable for the main program – a possibility sometimes overlooked, but which can often save time in the long run.

If the data is captive but not in machine-readable form, for example hand-written or printed, then problems of *transcription* have to be faced. Strictly, these are the responsibility of the system designer, but quite possibly the pro-grammer is the same person, and in any case he has to be aware of the problems. These arise mainly from the possibility of transcription errors, amounting to a near certainty if the volume of input is at all high. Transcription can take the form of punching on cards or paper tape, offline preparation onto a magnetic medium, as in key-to-disk systems, on-line preparation by creating and editing a disk file for later use as input to the main program, and direct data entry systems including direct input from an interactive keyboard to the running program. In all cases potential errors must be guarded against and allowed for. In the offline cases this means careful attention to verification and checking of the prepared input, but this is not enough; programs must be designed to perform whatever validity checks are reasonably possible, including such mechanisms as check digits, format checks, counting of input items where appropriate, and so on. Space precludes detailed discussion of all the possible techniques and the circumstances where they are appropriate; for this see the relevant literature, such as Waters' *Introduction to Computer Systems Design.*

Validation checks by the program itself are necessary, or at least desirable, not only to detect residual transcription errors, but to detect errors in the recording of the captive data, meaning that it is still incorrect although correctly transcribed — for example, recording a working week of 445 hours instead of 45 hours. Stories are legion of final demands threatening legal action if a debt of £0.00 is not paid, or of bills for unnaturally large amounts, many due to fundamental errors in program design but some certainly due to input errors not caught by validation checks. The consequences of such errors are frequently unfortunate and have been tragic. Such checks can occur not just at the time of input, of course, but later on as a result of subsequent calculations, as when individual items are themselves reasonable but are inconsistent considered together (such as total number of hours worked 45, including 50 hours overtime). These merge imperceptibly into general checks on the validity and proper functioning of the program as a whole.

The same situation applies in the case of online preparation of a disk file, if a simple general-purpose editor is used; however, this method permits a special-purpose input program to be written which incorporates both checks for and recovery procedures after transcription errors, and some, if not all possible, validation checks. There is no reason why such a program should not be written in a different language (say, one whose definition or implementation allows detailed checks on formatting) from the one used for the main program. Many variations are possible, including straightforward input by a text editor but then a run through a validation program separate from the main program. In the case of direct input to a running (interactive) program, input error checks and recovery procedures (to avoid having to re-run the entire program because of one false input item) have to be incorporated in the main program itself, though the verification and validation checking can exploit the presence of human judgement at the interactive terminal, and therefore may not need to be as elaborate as for a batch run.

If the data is not captive, its capture is part of the system design problem, and the choice of input media may be wider. The same possibilities as for transcription exist, but also some others, at least in principle. The chosen method may be recording and then transcription, in which case (as with already-recorded captive data) it can be remarked that, in general, punched input should if possible be confined to low volume; otherwise key-to-disk or some similar offline method, or an online method, must be considered. (A possible exception exists if the data is being collected over a long period). However, it may be possible to avoid the transcription problem by recording directly in machine readable form. If by hand, possibilities are mark-sensed cards, pre-scored cards, or documents which can be read by an optical mark reader; it may be possible to exploit documents printed, say, with magnetic ink or in optically readable fonts. A low-cost possibility appropriate in some cases is simply to have punched cards prepared beforehand, and the recording simply consists of selecting the appropriate kind of card.

One of the most attractive possibilities, if it can be arranged, is for recording by direct keyboard entry, either to build up a disk file or to be immediately processed. In the commercial world this is becoming increasingly common in, for example, transaction processing systems and point-of-sale terminal systems, while in the scientific field a similar technique can be used for direct recording and processing of experimental data through a terminal in the laboratory.

Particularly in the scientific and industrial fields, such methods may not be adequate to cope with the data, either because of its speed of generation or because it has to be collected over a long period. In this case *data logging* or *online monitoring* systems can be considered. For data rates up to about 100 characters per second, or for long-period recording, simple paper tape punches driven from the experimental system, for example from a digital counter or an analogue-to-digital converter, are usually satisfactory and reasonably cheap. For faster rates (or as a quieter and more compact alternative) cassette magnetic tapes can be considered. For the highest speeds and volumes, half-inch magnetic tape (often driven by a small dedicated processor) or direct entry to an online monitoring processor come into consideration, the last of course offering the possibility of online control also, as mentioned previously under output. The criteria of appropriateness, availability, and cost for judging between these various possibilities are obvious enough and should not need to be spelled out.

It will have been seen in this discussion that the question of batch versus interactive is just as important for input as for output, and it is worth saying a little more about this particular choice. Interactive computing is very seductive, and those who have become 'hooked' to this mode of computer use are often very reluctant to think of using batch mode for anything. Nevertheless, interactive computing carries a fairly substantial overhead compared with batch computing, though human convenience and comfort are usually worth paying some overhead for. In some cases, interactive mode is clearly indicated, as when genuine man-machine interaction is an essential feature of the process, or when the instant response of interactive systems is required. An interactive program can exploit human judgement in decision-making, not just in input but during the run itself — for example, in determining whether the rate of convergence of a numerical process is fast enough, or how to deal with some exceptional condition.

In a batch program, what has to be done needs to be determined in advance. Thus the same problem can often be solved legitimately by using either approach, but the solution is likely to be very different in form in the two cases. This will include both handling of input-output and the decision-making structure of the program.

Certainly there is little point in writing an interactive program without trying to exploit the judgement of the human user, even if its primary purpose is to obtain instant response. Nevertheless, this is what some devotees of interactive computing do, confusing the advantages of interactive *development* of a program with those of interactive *running*; it is certainly possible in many systems to develop interactively a program which in production will be run in batch mode. It is also possible that a program may be separable into sections which are more suitable for interactive working and sections which are more suitable for batch, or at least for which interaction is unnecessary. As indicated earlier, one example is a program for which human involvement in vetting input is desirable, but which then involves heavy processing and large volume output without any necessity for human guidance. It is simply pointless in such cases to keep an interactive terminal in contact with the program, except in those few cases when it is essential to output to that terminal despite the large volume, or to signal that the output is ready if it really is needed urgently. In short, the approach should be to match the mode of processing as well as the input-output methods to the needs of the problem, within the facilities available, rather than through habit, or a partiality to a particular approach whether or not it is the most suitable.

This section has once again demonstrated the interdependence of the various factors which have to be taken into account in a programming project. Input-output cannot be considered in isolation, or even only in conjunction with the computer systems available, since decisions about it are closely linked with decisions about the programming languages or packages to be used, and with the algorithmic design of the program.

Brian Meek

2.4 STRUCTURED PROGRAMMING

Now, at last, we turn to the actual program writing itself. Beginners may be surprised that it appears so far from the beginning of the book, but the earlier sections should have made clear why this should be.

Nowadays most programmers are aware that programs ought to be 'structured' without necessarily knowing quite what this means or how to achieve it. The term **structured programming** first came into prominence with the book of that title, by Dahl, Dijkstra and Hoare, published in 1972. Since then it has been widely used, in a number of different senses and without any consistent definition. Here we shall take it to mean a method of programming that leads to programs whose structure is clearly visible and is closely related to the structure of the problem that the program seeks to solve.

The move towards structured programming is often taken as dating from Dijkstra's famous letter that was published in 1968 with the heading 'GO TO statement considered harmful'. However, those who read that letter will find that he was not just stating that he had found it to be harmful — the mere fact had been known to Algol programmers long before — but that he had devised a good explanation of *why* it was harmful. A much better reference for the start of the movement is Naur's 1963 article 'Go to statements and good ALGOL style', where the point is well made that intelligent use of the **if-then-else** and **for-do** constructions will meet most requirements with greater clarity than will labels and **goto**s.

It is a well-known fact in manufacturing that it is a hopeless task to try to 'inspect good quality into a product'. While inspection is essential, the only place that the good quality can be inserted is on the production line. The same is true of computer programs. Testing and debugging are very inefficient and un-certain processes compared with writing a program correctly in the first place. Dijkstra clearly shows that, in general, it is impossible within the lifetime of the machine to test every possible case, and hence that 'Program testing can be used to show the presence of bugs, but never to show their absence'. The aim of structured programming is to try to make it a little easier to write programs correctly.

Let us look at seven principles of programming, while not seeking to deny that others might be added to the list.

1. **No tricks or 'clever' programming.** Never use a complicated method where a simple one would do. This principle has already been exemplified in Section 1.3.

2. **Few, if any, jumps.** It should not be thought that 'goto-less programming' is identical to 'structured programming'. It is possible to write a program without any jumps which nevertheless lacks logical structure. Conversely, there are situations that occasionally occur where a jump is the neat, simple, and straightforward thing to do, while other approaches are relatively obscure. One should not become so hidebound in one's ways as then to refuse the simple option.

   Even in a language such as Fortran (1966 standard version) where jumps cannot altogether be avoided, because of the lack of an **if-then-else** construction, reasonable care can avoid some of the 'logical spaghetti' that arises from thoughtless jumping. Thus

```
      IF (K .EQ. 3) GO TO 50
      A = B
      GO TO 60
   50 A = C
   60 .....(next statement)
```

is better written as

```
A = B
IF (K .EQ. 3) A = C
```

It can be argued that the latter version is less efficient on the machine as it sometimes assigns B to A when the operation is superfluous, but the amount of time so wasted is likely to be much less than the amount saved if this version requires less testing.

The reason for the greater simplicity is not so much that the second version is shorter, as that it contains no statement labels. Thus the flow of control is clear; it can enter only at the top and exit from the bottom. In the first version, on the other hand, the whole program unit needs to be searched to see whether GOTO 50 or GOTO 60 occurs anywhere, before the flow can be understood.

The problem is much more severe when trying to understand a program in Basic, because *every* line has to be numbered, and can be 'gone to' from any other line. Thus no passage can ever be looked at in the knowledge that it will never be entered in the middle.

3. **Choice, using if-then-else.** The object here is again to keep the flow of control simple, without any possibility of a jump into the structure from elsewhere. In Fortran, with no IF-THEN-ELSE available, you may have to write something like

```
      IF (K .LE. 1) GO TO 20
      A = B
      C = D
      GO TO 30
   20 A = F
      C = H
   30 ......(next statement)
```

but in Algol 60 it is much better to write

```
if K>1 then
        begin
        A:=B; C:=D
        end
    else
        begin
        A:=F; C:=H
        end
```

and the flow of control is clear.

Where the language allows conditional expressions, as well as conditional statements, these should be used, whenever they easily can, inside an expression rather than assigning to a variable and then using that variable in an expression. Thus in Fortran it might be necessary to write

```
A = C
IF (J .LT. 4) A = B
D = SQRT(A)
```

whereas in Algol it would be much better to write

$$D:=sqrt \text{ (if } J<4 \text{ then } B \text{ else } C)$$

The great advantage here is that one can see at a glance that the sole object is to assign a value to D, whereas in the first version part of the object might be to assign to A as well. Of course, sometimes it *is* desired to assign to A also – there is then no objection to the first sort of construction.

4. **Simple loops.** Backward jumps within a program nearly always turn out to be representable as some form of loop, and the flow of control can be made much clearer by so expressing them. There appears to be a school of thought, however, that allows only loops of the **while-do** and **repeat-until** types to count as 'structured', and to disallow loops such as the Fortran DO that step a controlled variable through a series of values. Thus Dijkstra in *Structured Programming* uses loops such as

$$k := 0; \textbf{ while } k<1000 \textbf{ do begin } statements; k := k+1 \textbf{ end}$$

But this is surely more complicated, less direct, and much more likely to lead to errors than

$$\textbf{for } k := 0 \textbf{ step } 1 \textbf{ until } 999 \textbf{ do } statements$$

which clearly expresses what is wanted in a simple and easy-to-get-right form.

This is not to deny that the **while** type of loop is exceedingly useful in its right place. Its lack is a serious disadvantage in languages that do not have it. We need each tool for use when appropriate.

5. **Segmentation.** A lengthy program that consists solely of a main program is usually quite unreadable. In the absence of an **if-then-else** construction it has to be full of labels and jumps, and the structure cannot be clear. If an **if-then-else** structure is available, and used, the depth of nesting is likely to become so great that the matching of an **else** to its corresponding **if-then** becomes difficult.

To avoid such difficulties every large program should be divided into a series of modules or procedures (subroutines and functions) so designed that each does a clearly defined task, is a logical part of the original problem, and so far as possible uses only its own, locally defined variables. Do not try to divide a program into *equal* chunks – 'chunks' will almost certainly be an apt word if you do – but into logical sections. Some of these may turn out to be small enough that they can remain as they are. Others will themselves need further division into an additional level of procedures, and so on.

The aim throughout should be that each module should be simple enough, both in itself and in its relation to the others, for it to be possible to test it independently. This is not at all an easy aim to satisfy, but constantly striving towards it can eventually bring great benefits in the final product. Further advice on this will be found in Section 3.1, where program development and testing are discussed.

6. **Recursion.** A delicate judgement is needed in deciding when to use recursion, as already mentioned in the last chapter. Anything that can easily be programmed as a simple loop usually should be, but in the right place recursion is so simple to specify that the user can hardly get it wrong. All the complicated 'housekeeping' that is needed, to keep track of the operations, is handed over to the machine to look after. It does depend, however, on using a language which permits recursion. For a detailed discussion see Section 1.3.

7. **Meaningful identifiers.** There is a tendency among most of us to be lazy, especially those of us with mathematical training, and to fall into the habit of algebra in using single letters to identify variables. Where we could write

$$velocity := initial\ velocity + acceleration \times time$$

we fall back on

$$v := u + a \times t$$

In this particular case, a user of the equations of motion is likely to be so used to v, u, a and t with these meanings that they are just as meaningful to him as the full words, but in the majority of programming tasks this is not so.

If using Basic, one may be compelled to use such abbreviated names, and nothing can be done about it; if using Fortran, the names must be reduced to not more than 6 characters, and it is not always easy to keep them meaningful. In a language that allows long names, the temptation to keep them short is always present. At the time that the program is being written it seems so much quicker and simpler, but when one wishes to modify a program a year after it was written, the extra ease of understanding given by meaningful names well repays all the effort of using them.

A further advantage occurs when a program is kept on a computer file, and may be changed by the use of an editing program. If you wish to find every use of TIME and change it to TIME1, because a new variable TIME2 is also being introduced, this is simple to do automatically, where to find every use of the variable T and change it to T1 is extremely difficult, as you do not wish to change RETURN to RET1URN, etc., in the process.

Even if variables are given abbreviated names, an attempt should be made to use meaningful ones for procedures. A program full of statements like

```
CALL ABC105(X, Y, 10)
```

is much more difficult to disentangle than one that uses

```
CALL MATINV(X, Y, 10)
```

even though MATINV is itself only an abbreviation of MATrix INVersion, and even though one may know why the (imaginary) ABC library of subroutines prefers the first sort of name. The 'CALL ABC105' type of statement should, at least, be accompanied by a comment whenever practicable.

With the help of these seven principles it should be much easier to write programs that are correct, understandable, and maintainable. If you are writing a program that will not fit with these principles, it almost certainly means that you do not understand well enough what you are seeking to do. This applies particularly if you are trying to understand someone else's program: if you cannot get the structure to behave itself, further study of the problem that it is trying to solve is likely to be useful.

We end this section by looking in detail at two examples. Reading programs, as opposed to writing them, is a somewhat underrated skill, but its regular exercise, as well as improving understanding of programming, rapidly leads the reader to appreciate the value of well-structured, intelligible programs. The examples chosen are ones which are good in their own way, as there would be little interest in trying to clarify examples starting as complete rubbish; we shall see instead how the application of the principles outlined above can help to improve programming which was not at all bad to begin with.

The first example is shown in Fig. 2.4A, and is taken from Algol 60 *Revised Report* published in 1962. It is a good piece of programming for its date, especially because it was written before any Algol 60 compiler was available, yet ran successfully when it was eventually tested.

procedure $RK(x, y, n, FKT, eps, eta, xE, yE, fi)$;
   value x, y ; **integer** n ;
Boolean fi ; **real** x, eps, eta, xE ; **array** y, yE ;
   procedure FKT ;
   comment : RK integrates the system

$$y'_k = f_k(x, y_1, y_2, \ldots, y_n) \quad (k = 1, 2, \ldots n)$$

of differential equations with the method of Runge-Kutta with automatic search for appropriate length of integration step. Parameters are: The initial values x and $y[k]$ for x and the unknown functions $y_k(x)$. The order n of the system. The procedure $FKT(x, y, n, z)$ which represents the system to be integrated, i.e. the set of functions f_k. The tolerance values eps and eta which govern the accuracy of the numerical integration. The end of the integration interval xE. The output parameter yE which represents the solution at $x = xE$. The Boolean variable fi, which must always be given the value **true** for an isolated or first entry into RK. If, however, the functions y must be available at several meshpoints $x_0, x_1, \ldots, x_n$, then the procedure must be called repeatedly (with $x = x_k$, $xE = x_{k+1}$, for $k = 0, 1, \ldots, n - 1$) and then the later calls may occur with $fi =$ **false** which saves computing time. The input parameters of FKT must be x, y, n, the output parameter z represents the set of derivatives $z[k] = f_k(x, y[1], y[2], \ldots, y[n])$ for x and the actual y's. A procedure comp enters as a non-local identifier ;

begin
   array $z, y1, y2, y3[1 : n]$; **real** $x1, x2, x3, H$;
     Boolean out ;
   integer k, j ; **own real** s, Hs ;
   procedure $RK1ST(x, y, h, xe, ye)$; **real** x, h, xe ;
     array y, ye ;
   comment : $RK1ST$ integrates one single RUNGE-KUTTA step with initial values $x, y[k]$ which yields the output parameters $xe = x + h$ and $ye[k]$, the latter being the solution at xe. IMPORTANT: the parameters n, FKT, z enter $RK1ST$ as non-local entities ;

begin
   array $w[1 : n], a[1 : 5]$; **integer** k, j ;
   $a[1] := a[2] := a[5] := h/2$; $a[3] := a[4] := h$;
   $xe := x$;
   for $k := 1$ **step** 1 **until** n **do** $ye[k] := w[k] := y[k]$;
   for $j := 1$ **step** 1 **until** 4 **do**
   begin
     $FKT(xe, w, n, z)$;
     $xe := x + a[j]$;
     for $k := 1$ **step** 1 **until** n **do**
     begin
       $w[k] := y[k] + a[j] \times z[k]$;
       $ye[k] := ye[k] + a[j + 1] \times z[k]/3$
     end k
   end j
  end $RK1ST$;

BEGIN OF PROGRAM:
   if fi **then begin** $H := xE - x$; $s := 0$ **end**
   else $H := Hs$; out := **false** ;

AA: **if** $(x + 2.01 \times H - xE > 0) \equiv (H > 0)$ **then**
   begin $Hs := H$; out := **true** ; $H := (xE - x)/2$
   end if ;
   $RK1ST(x, y, 2 \times H, x1, y1)$;

BB: $RK1ST(x, y, H, x2, y2)$; $RK1ST(x2, y2, H, x3, y3)$;
   for $k := 1$ **step** 1 **until** n **do**
     if $comp(y1[k], y3[k], eta) > eps$ **then go to** CC ;
   comment : $comp(a, b, c)$ is a function designator, the value of which is the absolute value of the difference of the mantissae of a and b, after the exponents of these quantities have been made equal to the largest of the exponents of the originally given parameters a, b, c ;
   $x := x3$; **if** out **then go to** DD ;
   for $k := 1$ **step** 1 **until** n **do** $y[k] := y3[k]$;
   if $s = 5$ **then begin** $s := 0$; $H := 2 \times H$ **end** if ;
   $s := s + 1$; **go to** AA ;

CC: $H := 0.5 \times H$; out := **false** ; $x1 := x2$;
   for $k := 1$ **step** 1 **until** n **do** $y1[k] := y2[k]$;
   go to BB ;

DD: **for** $k := 1$ **step** 1 **until** n **do** $yE[k] := y3[k]$
end RK

Fig. 2.4A – Runge-Kutta procedure from the Algol 60 Revised Report (1962)

Before looking at how this example can be improved, it is worth noting some good points:

1. The separation from each other, and from the body of the main procedure, of the two procedures *RK1ST* and *comp*. (Note: the text of *comp* is not given, being somewhat machine-dependent).
2. The extensive use of comment and the quality of the explanation which this provides.
3. The clear structure and layout of the body of the procedure *RK1ST*, which could hardly be improved.

The points which are open to criticism are the following:

1. In the main procedure *RK*, only the formal parameters x and y are shown as being called by value, whereas in fact n, eps, eta, xE and fi can and should also be called by value. Similarly in the local procedure *RK1ST*, x and h should be called by value. (This is a point rather specific to Algol 60).
2. The **own real** variable s would be better declared as **own integer**, particularly since the test 'if $s=5$' is being made. It is bad practice to assume that a 'real' value is ever known precisely, without rounding error.
3. In the main procedure *RK* a variable j is declared but never used (Note: for those unfamiliar with Algol 60, this j is not the same as the j declared and used within the procedure *RK1ST*). This is poor practice in any language.
4. After the end of the declaration of *RK1ST*, there is a label *BEGIN OF PROGRAM*. The use of (meaningful) labels merely for comment, as here, is not good practice. At the time the idea of meaningful labels was relatively novel and this kind of use was envisaged, before the potentially harmful nature of statement labels was properly recognized. Also (and this does not come from hindsight) the comment is unnecessary and, furthermore, untrue because what follows is a procedure body, not a program.
5. Most important from our point of view, the structure and layout of the body of the main procedure *RK* is abysmally bad — extraordinarily so in view of the quality of *RK1ST*.

As far as layout is concerned, it is almost sufficient to compare that of the body of *RK1ST* with that of the main procedure. For example, had the first two lines following *BEGIN OF PROGRAM* been written in the style of *RK1ST*, they could well have appeared as

```
if fi then begin
          H := xE − x;  s := 0
        end
     else H := Hs;
  out := false;
```

which is admittedly five lines instead of two, but much clearer.

However, it is the structure more than the layout of what follows which causes confusion, because the presence of labels and **goto** statements effectively obscures for the reader what the actual flow of control will be when the program is running. Ideally one would like to eliminate all four labels *AA, BB, CC, DD* and rewrite the text as something like (omitting the comments here for brevity)

```
while not out do
    begin
    if x + 2.01 × H − xE > 0 ≡ H > 0 then
        begin
        Hs := H;  out := true;  H := (xE − x)/2
        end;
    RK1ST(x, y, 2 × H, x1, y1);
    test := true;
    while test do
        begin
        RK1ST(x, y, H, x2, y2,);  RK1ST(x2, y2, H, x3, y3);
        k := 1;
        repeat
            begin
            test := comp(y1[k], y3[k], eta) > eps;
            if test then
                begin
                H := 0.5 × H;  out := false;  x1 := x2;
                for j := 1 step 1 until n do y1[j] := y2[j]
                end;
            k := k + 1
            end
        until k > n or test
        end test loop;
    x := x3;
    if not out then
        begin
        for k := 1 step 1 until n do y[k] := y3[k];
        if s ‡ 5 then s := s + 1 else
            begin
            s := 1;  H := 2 × H
            end
        end
    end not out loop;
    for k := 1 step 1 until n do yE[k] := y3[k]
    end RK
```

This is less compact than the original, but well worth it for the extra clarity, in showing where there are loops within loops, etc., of which the original gives no hint. It requires the declaration of *test* as an extra Boolean variable.

Unfortunately it is not quite Algol 60! As a minor point, **not, and** and **or** have been used instead of the symbols ⌐, ∧ and ∨ for the sake of extra clarity to those who are not used to the symbols. More importantly, it uses the constructions

> **while not** *out* **do** . . . .

and **while** *test* **do** . . .

It is a major deficiency of Algol 60 that these are not allowed without a corresponding **for**. Declaring *dummy* as an extra integer variable, they may be rewritten

> **for** *dummy* := 1 **while not** *out* **do** . . .

and **for** *dummy* := 1 **while** *test* **do** . . .

where at least the name gives the hint that the assignment to *dummy* is not really wanted.

Furthermore, the **repeat** . . . **until** construction is not available. To put it into Algol 60 we shall have to use

> **for** k := 1, $k + 1$ **while** $k \leqslant n$ **and** *test* **do**

instead, which some advocates of 'structured programming' would certainly not view favourably.

The fully rewritten form of this example appears in Fig. 2.4B. Note that j is still declared in spite of criticism 3 above, as it is now used.

---

procedure $RK(x,y,n,FKT,eps,eta,xE,yE,fi)$;
value, x,y,n,eps,eta,xE,fi;
integer n;   **Boolean** fi;   **real** x,eps,eta,xE;
array y,yE;   **procedure** FKT;
comment: *RK integrates the system*

$$y'_k = f_k(x, y_1, y_2, \ldots, y_n)\,(k = 1, 2, \ldots n)$$

of differential equations with the method of Runge-Kutta with automatic search for appropriate lengths of integration step. Parameters are: The initial values x and y[k] for x and the unknown functions $y_k(x)$. The order n of the system. The procedure FKT(x, y, n, z) which represents the system to be integrated, i.e. the set of functions f_k. The tolerance values eps and eta which govern the accuracy of the numerical integration. The end of the integration interval xE. The output parameter yE which represents the solution at x = xE. The Boolean variable fi, which must always be given the value **true** *for an isolated or first entry into RK. If, however, the functions y must be available at several meshpoints $x_0, x_1, \ldots, x_n$, then the procedure must be called repeatedly (with $x = x_k$, $xE = x_{k+1}$, for k =0, 1, ..., n − 1) and then the later calls may occur with fi =* **false** *which saves computing time. The input parameters of FKT must be x, y, n, the output parameter z represents the set of derivatives z[k] = $f_k(x, y[1], y[2], \ldots, y[n])$ for x and the actual y's. A procedure comp enters as a non-local identifier;*

```
begin array z, y1, y2, y3 [1:n] ;
real x1, x2, x3, H;  Boolean out, test;
integer k, j, dummy;  own real Hs;  own integer s;

procedure RK1ST(x, y, h, xe, ye);
value x, h;  real x, h, xe;  array y, ye;
```
comment: *RK1ST integrates one single RUNGE-KUTTA step with initial*
values x, y [k] which yields the output parameters xe = x + h and ye[k],
the latter being the solution at xe. IMPORTANT: the parameters n, FKT,
z enter RK1ST as non-local entities;
```
begin
array w[1:n] ,a[1:5] ;  integer k,j;
a[1] :=a[2] :=a[5] :=h/2;  a[3] :=a[4] :=h;
xe:=x;
for k:=1 step 1 until n do ye[k] :=w[k] :=y[k] ;
for j := 1 step 1 until 4 do
      begin
      FKT (xe,w,n,z);
      xe := x+a[j] ;
      for k := 1 step 1 until n do
            begin
            w[k]  :=y[k] +a[j]×z[k] ;
            ye[k]  :=ye[k] +a[j+1]×z[k] /3
            end k loop
      end j loop
end RK1ST;

if fi then
      begin
      H :=xE–x;  s:=0
      end
else H :=Hs;
out := false;
for dummy := 1 while ¬out do
      begin
      if x+2.01×H–xE>0≡H>0 then
            begin
            Hs :=H;  out := true;  H :=(xE–x)/2
            end;
      RK1ST(x,y,2×H,x1,y1);
      test := true;
      for dummy := 1 while test do
            begin
```

```
RK1ST(x,y,H,x2,y2); RK1ST(x2,y2,H,x3,y3);
for k := 1,k+1 while k<n ∧ ¬test do
    begin
    comment: comp(a, b, c) is a function designator, the value of
    which is the absolute value of the difference of the mantissae
    of a and b, after the exponents of these quantities have been
    made equal to the largest of the exponents of the originally
    given parameters a, b, c;
    test := comp(y1[k],y3[k], eta)>eps;
    if test then
        begin
        H := 0.5×H;  out := false;  x1 := x2;
        for j := 1 step 1 until n do y1[j] := y2[j]
        end
    end k loop
end dummy loop;

x := 3;
if ¬out then
    begin
    for k := 1 step 1 until n do y[k] :=y3[k];
    if s ≠ 5 then s :=s+1 else
        begin
        s :=1; H:=2×H
        end
    end
end dummy loop;
for k :=1 step 1 until n do yE[k]  :=y3[k]
end RK
```

Fig. 2.4B – Rewritten form of the Algol 60 procedure shown in Fig. 2.4A.

The second example comes from the algorithms section of *Applied Statistics* and is an algorithm by M. J. R. Healy, written as a Fortran subroutine, for finding a generalized inverse of a symmetric matrix. It is shown in Fig. 2.4C.

```
      SUBROUTINE SYMINV (A,N,C,W,NULLTY,IFAULT)
C
C         ALGORITHM   AS 7  J.R.STATIST.SOC. C, (1968)  VOL.17, NO.2.
C
C         FORMS IN C( ) AS LOWER TRIANGLE, A GENERALISED INVERSE
C         OF THE POSITIVE SEMI-DEFINITE SYMMETRIC MATRIX A( )
C         ORDER N, STORED AS LOWER TRIANGLE.
C         C( ) MAY COINCIDE WITH A( ).  NULLTY IS RETURNED AS THE NULLITY
C         OF A( ).  IFAULT IS RETURNED AS 1 IF N.LT.1, OTHERWISE ZERO.
C         W( ) IS A WORK ARRAY OF LENGTH AT LEAST N THAT IS ALLOCATED BY
C         THE CALLING ROUTINE.
C
C
      DIMENSION A(1),C(1),W(1)
C
      NROW = N
      IFAULT = 1
      IF (NROW.LE.0)  GO TO 100
      IFAULT = 0
      CALL CHOL (A,NROW,C,NULLTY,IFAULT)
      IF (IFAULT.NE.0) GO TO 100
      NN = (NROW*(NROW+1))/2
      IROW = NROW
      NDIAG = NN
   16 IF (C(NDIAG).EQ.0.0) GO TO 11
      L = NDIAG
      DO 10 I = IROW,NROW
      W(I) = C(L)
      L = L + I
   10 CONTINUE
      ICOL = NROW
      JCOL = NN
      MDIAG = NN
   15 L = JCOL
      X = 0.0
      IF (ICOL.EQ.IROW) X = 1.0/W(IROW)
      K = NROW
   13 IF (K.EQ.IROW) GO TO 12
      X = X - W(K)*C(L)
      K = K - 1
      L = L - 1
      IF (L.GT.MDIAG) L = L - K + 1
      GO TO 13
```

```
   12 C(L) = X/W(IROW)
      IF (ICOL.EQ.IROW) GO TO 14
      MDIAG = MDIAG - ICOL
      ICOL = ICOL - 1
      JCOL = JCOL - 1
      GO TO 15
   11 L = NDIAG
      DO 17 J = IROW,NROW
      C(L) = 0.0
      L = L + J
   17 CONTINUE
   14 NDIAG = NDIAG - IROW
      IROW = IROW - 1
      IF (IROW.NE.0) GO TO 16
  100 RETURN
      END
```

Fig. 2.4C – M. J. R. Healy's Fortran subroutine to invert a symmetric matrix.

It does its job correctly and efficiently. This is the most important thing, and no questions of structure can possibly overcome the need for that. But it is certainly far from clear at a glance what paths may be taken through the algorithm. (You might, perhaps, like to see how long it takes you to spot the instruction that appears twice that could equally well appear once only!)

This subroutine can be criticized for the following features:

1. The DIMENSION statement is not in Standard Fortran since it uses the 'dummy 1' for the dimension bound (see discussion in Section 2.2). To correct this means passing NN as well as N as an argument instead of calculating it internally.

2. The comment says that C( ) may coincide with A( ), but this is prohibited by the Fortran standard.

3. The label numbers are out of order. This does not matter to the machine; nor does it matter much to the human for an algorithm of this length, but for longer algorithms it matters very much to a human who wishes to follow it easily. ('GOTO 12 – now where on earth is 12?' Hunting for it is so frustrating and so unnecessary).

4. The comment does not say what CHOL does. (However, where SYMINV was originally published CHOL was the previous algorithm in the journal, and it was mentioned in the introductory text; taking the one algorithm out of context like this is not really fair!)

5. CHOL also needs NN as an extra argument if it is to meet the Fortran standard.

6. The comment does not mention that IFAULT may return as 2, since CHOL can give it this value.
7. Two counting variables, I and J, are used where one would do.
8. No use is made of indenting to clarify the structure; however, arguments can be made against indentation in Fortran — see *Applied Statistics* **24**, 1975, p. 368 — and even if an author submits with indentation this journal will remove it.

The criticisms are minor compared with the worth of the algorithm; the more important criticism, of lack of apparent structure, is much more the fault of the Fortran language than of the author of the algorithm. Fig. 2.4D shows the algorithm translated into Algol 60, where the structure is clearer. (The structure could probably be made clearer still in, say, Pascal or Algol 68, but it was preferred to have only two different languages in this section).

```
procedure syminv (a, n, c, nullity, ifault);
value n; integer n, nullity, ifault; real array a, c;
if n<1 then ifault := 1 else
begin
chol(a, n, c, nullity, ifault);
if ifault = 0 then
     begin integer j, k, l, icol, jcol, irow, nn, ndiag, mdiag;
     real x; real array w[1 :n] ;
     nn := ndiag := n × (n + 1) ÷ 2;
     for irow := n step − 1 until 1 do
          begin
          if c [ndiag]  = 0.0 then
               begin
               l := ndiag;
               for j := irow step 1 until n do
                    begin
                    c [l]  := 0.0; l := l + j
                    end j loop
               end
          else
               begin
               l := ndiag;
               for j := irow step 1 until n do
                    begin
                    w [j]  := c [l] ; l := l + j
                    end j loop;
```

```
            jcol := nn;
            j := irow + 1;
            mdiag := nn + 1;
            for icol := n step −1 until irow do
                begin
                l := jcol;
                x := if icol = irow then 1.0/w[irow] else 0.0;
                for k := n step −1 until j do
                    begin
                    x := x − w[k] × c[l];
                    l := l − (if l > mdiag then k − 1 else 1)
                    end k loop;
                c[l] := x/w[irow];
                if icol ≠ irow then
                    begin
                    mdiag := mdiag − icol;
                    jcol := jcol − 1
                    end
                end icol loop
            end c[ndiag] ≠ 0.0;
        ndiag := ndiag − irow
        end irow loop
    end block
end syminv
```

Fig. 2.4D − The Fortran subroutine of Fig. 2.4C translated into Algol 60.

The comment has been omitted from the translation for the sake of brevity. It is not suggested that it should be omitted in practice. The identifiers have been left much the same to allow easy comparisons.

The instruction that appears twice is much clearer in this version. After the test **if** $c[ndiag] = 0.0$ the next thing to be done is $l := ndiag$ whichever way the test goes. It could be inserted once only, immediately before the test. In this version it is clear that this can be done with no fear of upsetting anything, whereas in the original it is necessary to hunt through the whole algorithm to see whether there is another GOTO 11 anywhere before it is known to be safe. A minor matter? Yes, but it is the cumulative effect of the repetition of such minor matters over and over again that gives the structured approach much of its power.

It can now be seen from Fig. 2.4D that the algorithm consists largely of a sequence of loops many of which count downwards. This shows why the original could not be constructed of a simple sequence of DO-loops: the Fortran DO-loop is allowed only to count upwards. It is possible, however, to introduce a variable to count upwards and serve no other purpose, while the variable one really wishes to use counts downwards within the loop.

Has this analysis helped to clarify the original? It is suggested that it has, and that the rewritten version in Fig. 2.4E is consequently easier to understand, and easier to modify with confidence should any modification be required.

I. D. Hill

```
      SUBROUTINE SYMINV (A, N, NN, C, W, NULLTY, IFAULT)
C
C
C         FORMS IN C( ) AS LOWER TRIANGLE, A GENERALISED INVERSE
C         OF THE POSITIVE SEMI-DEFINITE SYMMETRIC MATRIX A( )
C         ORDER N, STORED AS LOWER TRIANGLE.
C
C         NULLTY IS RETURNED AS THE NULLITY OF A.
C         IFAULT IS RETURNED AS 1 IF N .LT. 1 .OR. NN .LT. 1
C                               2 IF A IS NOT POSITIVE SEMI-DEFINITE
C                               3 IF NN .NE. N * (N+1) / 2
C                               0 OTHERWISE.
C         W( ) IS A WORK ARRAY OF LENGTH AT LEAST N.
C         CHOL IS A SUBROUTINE FOR THE TRIANGULAR DECOMPOSITION OF
C         THE MATRIX.
C
      DIMENSION A(NN), C(NN), W(N)
      IFAULT = 1
      IF (N .LT. 1 .OR. NN .LT. 1) RETURN
      IFAULT = 3
      IF (NN .NE. N * (N + 1) / 2) RETURN
C
      CALL CHOL(A, N, NN, C, NULLTY, IFAULT)
      IF (IFAULT .NE. 0) RETURN
      NDIAG = NN
      IROW = N + 1
      DO 60 IW = 1, N
        IROW = IROW - 1
        L = NDIAG
        IF (C(NDIAG) .NE. 0.0) GO TO 20
        DO 10 J = IROW, N
          C(L) = 0.0
          L = L + J
10      CONTINUE
        GO TO 55
```

```
C
   20    DO 30 J = IROW, N
            W(J) = C(L)
            L = L + J
   30      CONTINUE
         JCOL = NN
         MDIAG = NN
         J = IROW + 1
         ICOL = N + 1
         DO 50 IL = IROW, N
            ICOL = ICOL - 1
            L = JCOL
            X = 0.0
            IF (ICOL .EQ. IROW) X = 1.0 / W(IROW)
            IF (J .GT. N) GO TO 45
            K = N
            DO 40 KK = J, N
               X = X - W(K) * C(L)
               K = K - 1
               L = L - 1
               IF (L .GT. MDIAG) L = L - K + 1
   40       CONTINUE
   45       C(L) = X / W(IROW)
            IF (ICOL .EQ. IROW) GO TO 50
            MDIAG = MDIAG - ICOL
            JCOL = JCOL - 1
   50      CONTINUE
C
   55    NDIAG = NDIAG - IROW
   60    CONTINUE
         RETURN
         END
```

Fig. 2.4E – Rewritten form of the Fortran subroutine shown in Fig. 2.4C.

CHAPTER 3

Program Development

One of the very first lessons learned in any introductory course on programming is that designing and constructing a program initially is by no means the end of the programming process. A program that is 'right first time' is the rare exception rather than the rule, in all but the most trivial of cases. A lesson learned less immediately is that errors will not necessarily be detected by the compiler, or be obvious from the output if the program 'works' in the sense that it compiles and runs. This chapter is therefore concerned with program development, the problems of getting a program from its initial state to a state which, if not final or completely error-free, is at least one in which the program is reasonably usable for the purpose for which it was designed. The first section deals with the important (though often underrated) matter of error *prevention*, continuing the theme of structured programming introduced at the end of the last chapter, with special emphasis on its value in reducing the incidence of errors, limiting their effects, and making them easier to detect if they do still occur. The second is concerned with techniques for detecting errors. The third and final section discusses a further aspect of program development, that of improving performance in ways other than the removal of errors; it also forms an introduction to several of the matters discussed in Chapter 4.

3.1 STRUCTURED PROGRAMMING AND ERROR PREVENTION

In the last section of the preceding chapter, structured programming was introduced and discussed mainly in terms of expressing algorithms in a programming language with the greatest possible clarity. It was, however, made clear that one of the primary reasons for adopting the technique was to reduce the incidence of errors, both by making the program text easier to understand and by making the program easier to test. Now that the principles have been laid down, and illustrated in fairly small-scale examples, we shall look further at the question of errors in programs, and at how the techniques of structured programming help us to cope with them, particularly in the case of very large programming projects.

Programmers are human beings, just like other people, and being human they are subject to human frailties. Thus, given that most programs are written by human beings, it is inevitable that they will contain errors; in other words, that they will not work correctly. In fact, with our present limited understanding of how best to build programs, it is almost certain that every program of significant size contains at least one undiscovered error, and computers are still unforgiving of our errors. Nevertheless, while it seems that we must accept the inevitability of errors, we need to be able both to build large systems and to rely on their continuing error-free operation. We must therefore use program building techniques which minimize the possibilities for errors, program testing methods which maximize the chances of finding errors, and program design methods which limit the effects of errors. The first step in this process is to recognize that errors can and do exist and, without a valid mathematical proof that the program is correct, will continue to exist. Since the correctness proofs of large programs are also large and complex, the possibility of errors in the proof cannot be ruled out; the possibility of errors remaining in the program exists. Techniques for proving the correctness of programs, and the associated problem of designing programming languages which assist such techniques, are the subject matter of an important current research area; but until that research bears fruit, and the fruit is widely available, practical programming requires the use of indirect methods to try to improve the reliability of software.

The process of minimizing the number of errors in a program follows a law of diminishing returns. Initially, a modest increase in effort will result in a marked decrease in the number of errors remaining in the program. Subsequently, more and more effort must be made to reduce − but not eliminate − this residue of errors. The process ends when the number of errors remaining is tolerable, and the limited damage which they can cause is insufficient to justify the costs of eliminating any more of them. All of this may sound somewhat defeatist, but it is the only sensible approach to adopt when perfection is not practicable to achieve. In fact, the rest of this section discusses techniques which help to reduce the incidence of errors and to improve the chances of their detection, hence improving the cost-effectiveness of program testing and debugging.

As in many other situations, prevention of the undesirable is more cost-effective than cure, and programs should therefore be written in such a way that the likelihood of errors is minimized, that such errors as remain will be easier to detect, and that the effects of the errors will be contained, that is, both minimized and restricted in range. It is necessary to take this into account at all four of the main stages in programming a project: specification, design, building, and testing, at any of which errors may be introduced.

As we have seen earlier, construction of every program or subprogram must start with a specification which describes how the program is to relate to the real world or a model of the real world. Ideally, and usually, this is a written document, and is used as the initial reference for all the construction work which follows. Sometimes, especially with small, informal programs, the specification is never explicitly set out but remains in the head of the programmer as a mental concept of what he has to do. There are two possibilities for error at this stage. Firstly, the initial specification may be faulty because it is not an accurate description of what the program is to do. This may be a consequence of a misunderstanding by the writer of the specification, or a flaw in the model of the real world that was used. Secondly, the programmer may misinterpret the specification. The result is the same in either case; the program will not perform the tasks required of it − it will solve the wrong problem.

The second stage, of designing a program to satisfy the given specification, can also introduce errors, obviously because the design does not match the specification, or more subtly because it will not function as required in all the circumstances asked of it. It is rather analogous to designing a machine which is perfect in theory, but requires 100% perfection in, say, input materials or op-erator control if it is to work satisfactorily in an imperfect world. Typical of this class of error is that a program malfunctions because the algorithm on which it is based cannot cope with an unexpected combination of input values from which it has not been protected. Most errors, however, arise at the building or coding stage. Errors from this stage can be divided into three main groups. The first group consists of logical errors arising because the programmer misunderstands the language used or the fine detail of the program. Examples of this kind of error are failure to initialize a variable, incorrect initialization of or exit from an iterative loop, and incorrect use of a variable. In the second group are syntax errors which result in code that is unacceptable to the compiler. These generally arise from carelessness in actual coding, but may reflect inadequate understanding of the programming language. In the third group are errors introduced between the programmer and the version of his program which reaches the computer. This group includes transcription and encoding errors, whereby what the pro-grammer intended to write differs from that which appears on the coding sheet or that which is keyed onto cards, tape, disk, or directly into the computer at a terminal. It also includes errors caused by mishandled punched cards, malfunctioning equipment, transmission faults, etc.

The final stage of production also has potential for introducing errors. Disorganized testing can, for example, lead to the use of out-of-date program listings, the wrong identification of errors and what must be done to correct them, and the incorrect amendment of the code. In the resulting confusion, the number of errors in the program can be significantly increased!

Prevention

At each of the four stages just discussed there are precautions that can be taken to minimize the possibility of errors. The first is to study the initial specification carefully and intelligently. Any peculiarities or ambiguities should be investigated, and unclear passages should be clarified. This will reduce the possibilities for errors and misunderstandings in the specification.

Much successful error prevention stems from the design process, in the selection of the algorithm and of the programming language and style, and from the structure of the design process itself. It has already been indicated that structured design, which implies using a top-down process, is inherently less prone to errors than bottom-up design or monolithic design, and it is time to explain why. The top-down, structured design process, illustrated in Fig. 3.1A, follows a cycle of specification, design, building and testing for each of the modules in the program. It starts with the specification and design of the main module. During the design of each module, its requirements for sub-modules become clear, and an exact functional specification can be written for each of these. This offers two main advantages. The specification for each module is fixed during the design process and need not be altered later. With a bottom-up approach, where the specification, design, building, and testing of modules begins at the lowest level, there is always a risk that the completed modules near the bottom of the hierarchy will have to be changed as design problems and changes are encountered higher up. The second advantage is in program testing. As we shall see later, it is usually easier to simulate the function of lower modules during the program validation, than to provide an accurate testing environment for an isolated module.

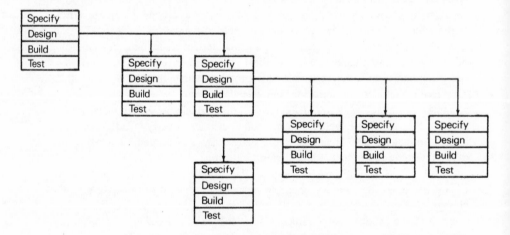

Fig. 3.1A — Structured (top down) design.

As we have seen in Section 1.3, in choosing the algorithm to be used in the program or module, the designer must take care that it will function correctly under all permissible conditions, and then ensure that it is protected from impermissible conditions by validating the data crossing the interface between this module and the rest of the program.

The design of resilient, error-resistant programs also has implications for the choice of programming language. Since the technique of structured programming, with its control over the program flow, reduces the possibility of errors in logic, ideally the language should lend itself to writing structured programs. It is well known that some languages, like Algol 68 and Pascal, have good constructs for expressing the flow of program control, and also allow the programmer to specify and manipulate data structures which reflect the requirements of the problem, whereas other languages, like Fortran and (even more) Basic, are very deficient in these respects. These matters have already been discussed in Sections 2.1 and 2.4. But the differences, as far as reliability and error control are concerned, do not end there. For example, many Fortran implementations are very tolerant of the ways in which typed variables are used. As one instance, a group of Hollerith characters can be stored in an integer variable and then assigned to a real variable with automatic mode conversion and little probability of the fact being signalled. It is unlikely that such a sequence would be programmed intentionally, but this error could slip through the net of prevention. Other languages, such as Algol 68, are more rigid about mode conversion and require explicit permission in cases where errors might occur. While it may seem tedious to be fettered by rules of scope and variable usage, it does enable many more errors to be detected by the compiler, leaving fewer to corrupt the program execution. Those errors which can be detected in this way are also those which can be particularly troublesome later.

However, as explained in Section 2.1, there are many factors to be taken into account when choosing a programming language, and it is often necessary to use one which is not ideal from this point of view. This is where programming style becomes especially important, even though a good style like that outlined in Section 2.4 is harder to maintain in languages unsympathetic to structured programming than in those that are. In any language a clear programming style is useful in preventing errors, because it makes the code clearer and easier to understand, and the errors are therefore easier to see. It also pays dividends later because, during the interval between writing and debugging the code, it is very easy to forget exactly how the program is intended to function.

The effects of errors can be reduced and their location determined by the practice of 'firewalling' and double checking within the program. Firewalling involves the checking of the parameters passed to the module through its interface, and protects the algorithm from impermissible input conditions. No matter that the calling module should never pass erroneous parameters; if something can go wrong, one day it will. If these parameters are checked for reasonableness and consistency, then the damage caused by the error cannot propagate through the program, and (for example) possible damage to precious files will be avoided. Further, the error will be determined sooner and therefore more accurately. There are often key points within a module where vulnerable variables should be checked. This serves the same purpose as firewalling, locating possible errors and minimizing damage.

Having reached the point where the module has been designed, the next stage is to build or code it. Most of the errors in this process are caused by carelessness or illegible writing. Coding is an exacting task, which should not be hurried. Coding conventions exist so that potentially similar characters can be distinguished, such as the letters O and I from the digits 0 and 1. Since, on some equipment, they also look very similar in the program listing, it is worth while getting them right initially. This may seem too trivial to mention, but many programmers have found to their cost that it does not pay to neglect it.

The code should now be checked, a process in which the computer can be used to complement but not replace the programmer. It is easier to check code from a clear listing with good layout. The importance of good layout was noted in Section 2.4, and is particularly valuable at this stage; some systems provide special layout programs or options to assist in this, providing appropriate indentations (and incidentally providing a check on the programmer's own indentations). Another useful machine-generated check is a table of the variables used in each module, showing where each is used and how it is used. The compiler may also carry out checks on variable usage and scope. In languages which require explicit declarations of all the variables, this can help to highlight misspelled variable names and incorrect usage. Invalid transfers of control, such as a branch into the middle of an iterative loop or conditional clause, can also be detected. This is where the choice of language and the compiler used has a significant impact on the early detection of errors. It is all too easy to be tempted to 'switch off' such compiler options (though such switching-off facilities are provided for use with fully-developed modules, not programs still under development) or to skimp or skip the task of examining them. Such temptations you should be strong-willed enough to resist if you wish to become a fully competent programmer!

Nevertheless, automatic checking, although useful, does not eliminate the need for desk checking by a programmer: 'a programmer' rather than 'the programmer' because any programmer is limited in his ability to check his own code. He is unlikely to detect any errors due to his own misunderstandings of the specification, of the algorithm, or of the language, because his understanding is unlikely to have improved during the writing of the program. Further, his familiarity with the code he is checking may lead him to overlook errors, however glaring they may be. It is therefore better if another person can desk check the code. There are two main techniques of 'programmer peer review', which is the jargon for this practice. In one, the programmers work in pairs, and each desk checks the modules written by the other. This may be extended so that modules are exchanged for the whole of the testing and debugging process. The other technique requires the programmer to explain his code to a group of other programmers, who then offer constructive criticism and point out possible errors. Both techniques offer additional advantages. Firstly, the review, especially if carried out on a group basis, can result in improvements to the module, to improve its accuracy, reliability, or efficiency. Secondly, the programming style diffuses and becomes more uniform throughout the organization. Good ideas are shared, and the intelligibility of the code is improved. Thirdly, because more programmers have studied each module, the problems of later maintenance are reduced: the organization is less dependent on the continuing availability of the original author. (See Section 5.4 for more discussion of working in a team.)

There are four specific questions that should be asked in desk checking:

1. Is the code both necessary and sufficient? Check that all the steps in the algorithm have been coded and that there are no redundant statements to confuse or produce errors.
2. Is all the non-local data used correctly? Check that the declaration, usage, and range of accepted values for each non-local variable is consistent with its use everywhere else.
3. Is the usage of local data consistent? Check that there are no unexpected variables, that each is used in a consistent way, and that the range of permitted values is acceptable.
4. Is each variable set before it is used? Check that the program does not assume an initial value for any variable, but explicitly sets a value, either at compile time or by assignment before it is used.

Even if you are perforce working alone, without even a friend whom you can ask to look at your program for you, it is worth going through this list as well as you can on your own code, trying as far as possible to pretend it was written by someone else. Mention was made in Section 1.1 of the value of trying to explain a problem to an imaginary audience, if a real one is not available; for desk checking, some programmers find that it helps to explain their coding to a non-existent colleague in a similar way.

                                                                    Nick Rushby

3.2 TESTING AND DEBUGGING

Testing

It is program testing, rather than debugging, which is the central feature of the final stage in the creation of a program. The objective of testing is to verify that the program functions as it should, that it conforms with its specification, and solves the right problem in the real world. This is an uncompromising goal, and is also measurable in that it is possible, at least in principle, to decide when it has been reached. The aim of program debugging, on the other hand, is to remove program errors, and does not necessarily have the same result as testing. Testing may throw up errors which have to be corrected; debugging, in the sense of dealing with errors as they become evident but otherwise 'leaving well alone', may leave at any stage some sections of program untested. Also, since the detection and location of program errors follows a law of diminishing returns, it is reasonable to stop error hunting when only a relatively small number of errors are left and the costs of finding any more are not justified. At this point, which can be difficult to determine, the program may still not function correctly under all conditions.

Ideally, the program should be tested with all possible combinations of input, and its output for each case checked against precalculated correct results. However, for almost all programs, even the simplest, there is an infinity of possible input combinations, or at least a number so large as to be effectively infinite. Consider, for example, a program to add three integers together. Each of the integers could range from positive to negative infinity, and hence the number of different input combinations is infinite. Even if the integers are limited to a reasonable range of values, say $\pm 8 \times 10^6$, there are still too many combinations to be checked by hand in a reasonable time. Sceptical readers are invited to carry out the calculations for themselves! Fortunately, the internal operations of the computer system can be considered to have generality: if they work with one set of operands then they will work, within certain limits, for all similar sets of operands. Less fortunately, the same assumption is not valid for programs or parts of programs which contain conditional branches. Testing must therefore be focused on the validation of small, separate parts of the program which do have this kind of generality. It may then be inferred that, if the small part performs correctly with one set of inputs, it will perform correctly with all others. The crux is to decide what constitutes a part simple enough to be validated in this way.

This requirement is provided by the notion of a program path — the sequence of instructions which is performed for a given set of inputs. If this works correctly, then all other sets of inputs which cause the program to follow the same path also yield the correct result. Since most programs contain conditional branches, there will be a number of alternative paths at various parts of the program, and hence very many distinct paths through the code. Exhaustive testing or validation of the program requires that each of these paths should be checked. The total number of paths is determined by the combination of all the alternatives at each stage. Although this is much less then infinity, it may still be unacceptably large for big programs. It is reduced to manageable size by breaking up the programs, validating each part separately, and then using the validated parts as single steps in a longer path. The concept of generality ensures that this technique is valid whatever the number of internal paths in the individual parts. The process is illustrated in Fig. 3.2A.

Such a method accords well with the techniques of structured design and programming which require that the program should be divided into logical and functional modules, as illustrated in Fig 3.1A. Each of these is validated individually but not in isolation. The testing, like overall construction, proceeds from the top downwards. At each successive stage, the functions of lower modules in the structure are simulated, while the module under test is exercised through all of its logical paths. The testing environment is illustrated in Fig. 3.2B. As the example in Fig. 3.2A demonstrates, the number of different tests which must be devised — one for each logical path — is largely determined by the sum of the number of paths in each module, instead of involving the products, the other important factor being the carry-over of values from one module to the next.

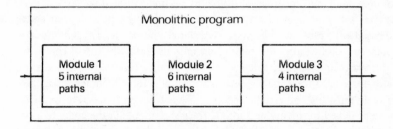

Fig. 3.2A — The number of distinct paths is 5 × 6 × 4 = 120 if the program is tested monolithically, but 5 + 6 + 4 = 15, plus one when the modules are linked and each is regarded as a single step — that is, 16 paths in all — if the program is divided into modules.

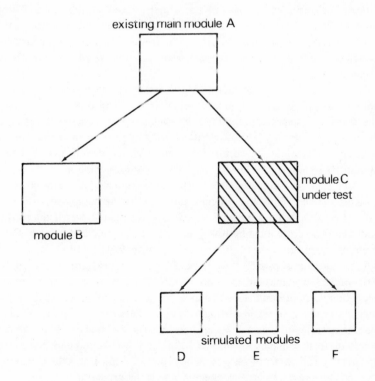

Fig. 3.2B — Module testing environment.

Testing of such a modular program starts with the main module in an environment where all the other modules are simulated. As each module is validated it can be added to the structure and its subordinate modules can be investigated. Thus the overall function of the program is apparent from the beginning, and any fundamental problems are uncovered at an early stage.

The test data used to drive each module through all its logical paths must be devised with care. In addition to data which should clearly cause the execution to follow a given path, the set should contain data which will check marginal conditions. For example, a decision point which tests whether a real value is greater than 1.0 should be checked with values greater than, less than, and equal to 1.0. It must also be established that the correct path has been followed. This can be achieved by including suitable trace statements in the code, to signal that a given path has been executed. Once the code has been validated, these can be removed or disabled. Some compilers offer facilities for 'debugging' statements which can be included or ignored according to the setting of some debugging 'switch', such as a job control card option. An alternative method of ensuring that all the code has been checked is to test the program while running under the control of a utility which counts the number of times each statement is executed. Such utilities ('profilers') are primarily used to measure and improve program efficiency, as is explained in the next section; but their output is used at the testing stage not to determine the most frequently used statements, but to show whether any statements have not been executed at all and have therefore not been tested.

The production of large quantities of test data can be eased by using the computer itself to format or generate suitable input. Test files of reasonable data can be written by a special program, or by a general purpose generator. Additional cases to test marginal conditions, critical code sequences and error conditions must be added. The 'correct' results for each set should then be determined. This is a potential source of confusion, for errors in the calculation of the expected results will lead the programmer to suspect the veracity of the program under test. After the test shot, the program output must be compared with the pre-calculated results. Any discrepancies must be investigated, and if the program is at fault then the error must be found and tested. Program testing ends when the program has been run successfully through all of its logical paths.

A programmer's capacity to write and test a program is limited by his experience and imagination; in other words, if he is unaware that, or cannot imagine that, certain conditions can arise, he will not allow for them when designing the program or when testing it. This applies also to misunderstandings in the initial specification. Lack of imagination is the probable cause of the famous instances of final demands for bills of £0.00, and the like; no-one realized that it could happen, and so no check was made. This again illustrates the advantages of having another programmer desk check and test the program.

The testing process is a certification of the program, and must be documented for future credibility. Future users of the program are entitled to more than an unsupported statement that the program works. They should know how and under what conditions it was tested, and what the inputs and results were, so that the tests can be repeated. (Retesting will certainly be necessary if the program is ever modified or transferred to another computer system.) The documentation should include details of the test procedures, the functions of each test set, the test data, and the calculated results.

Debugging

Knowing that errors exist is one thing; getting rid of them is quite another. The errors in a program or module may manifest themselves in a variety of ways. We have already considered those errors of syntax and internal consistency which can be detected by the compiler. There are also logical errors, broadly of two kinds. There are those which do not cause the program to fail, but cause discrepancies between the expected results and those which are actually produced; and there are those which result in illegal operations such as division by zero, attempting to read past the end of an input file, or attempting to access a non-existent array element, which lead to the premature termination of the program. The division between the two kinds is not clear-cut. In some languages and systems, for example, array bound checking at run-time is automatic, but in others it is not; a Fortran system will normally check array bounds only if this is asked for, if indeed it offers the facility at all. In this case an incorrect access may either result in a premature termination, if the location addressed is outside the range available to the program, or may simply lead to incorrect results. (In fact, if you are really unlucky, in a particular case it may not even do that, and the error will not manifest itself!) It is important to be aware of which such errors your compiler is capable of detecting, and to provide your own checks for those it will ignore. Also, some compilers incorporate 'recovery' facilities to permit continued processing if an exceptional condition like division by zero arises. If the compiler reports the unexpected occurrence of such a recovery, this must still of course be regarded as an error and treated accordingly.

The diagnosis of logical errors is complicated by the delay which normally exists between the occurrence of the actual error and the appearance of the symptoms. Although it is easy to locate the point at which the first incorrect output was printed or at which the run terminated with an execution error, the real error may have occurred some distance away and may not be so easy to find. The key to efficient debugging is the systematic exploration and elaboration of the symptoms, so that the precise cause of the error can be identified. This process starts with the collection of all the available evidence: what happened; to what extent it happened (if appropriate); when it happened; and where the symptoms appeared. Information about what did *not* happen is as important as the details of what did — as Sherlock Holmes pointed out in *The Hound of the Baskervilles*. From this evidence, the programmer can begin to formulate hypotheses about the cause of the error, and to devise tests of these hypotheses.

The single symptom which originally signalled the error will not usually yield sufficient information on its own; additional information must be extracted from the test run. However, beware of generating too much information, for the relevant facts will then be buried in a morass of useless figures. This, incidentally, is the main drawback of post-mortem dumps, which are often provided automatically by the operating system when a premature termination ('abort') occurs as the result of an illegal operation. Undue importance is often attached to the analysis of such dumps, which in most cases should be considered only as a last resort.

A better solution is to trace the execution of the program in the vicinity of the error. Some debugging compilers provide a trace, which can be used simply to follow the program flow from statement to statement, or can include details of each assignment, with the values of relevant expressions. Again there is a risk of producing too much data. The error might not occur until the test run is well advanced, after many thousands of statements have been executed, and several hundred pages of trace output have been printed. Usually the trace can be turned on or off for each module individually, and thus can be used to trace only the module under test. This reduces the output to a more manageable amount. Some compilers offer the option of including a retrospective trace of a program under test. In such systems the trace data is stored during the run in a cyclic buffer so that at any time the trace data is stored for, say, the last 100 statements. If an execution error occurs during the run, the contents of the trace buffer are printed. This provides information about the run in the moments before the catastrophic failure, which (with luck) will contain the prime cause of the error, or at least provide some clues as to its nature and location. It is possible (something which is sometimes overlooked) to press this facility into service even if the program terminates normally (hence producing no retrospective trace) but with incorrect results. The technique is to introduce deliberately an execution error before the end, at a point just past the suspected fault. A suitable statement, for example including an attempt to divide by zero, inserted in the code at the appropriate point, will force an error and generate the trace output. However, this is a once-only device which cannot easily be used to investigate errors occurring in a loop after a number of iterations.

Perhaps the most useful debugging tool is the 'snapshot', which produces a printout of selected variables at key points in the program. The printout may be achieved by a special debugging feature in the language, for example the namelist facility available in some Fortran systems, or more flexibly by print statements set up by the programmer. Again, beware of snapshots used in inner loops which may be executed very many times. If the working of an inner loop is to be investigated, the snapshot can be controlled by code which bypasses it after a small number of iterations, or only activates it after the loop has been executed a given number of times. The amount of detail printed by the snapshot is under the control of the programmer, and can range from a brief message that a given point has been passed, to an appropriately formatted display of the values of chosen variables. All the snapshots should print some identification so that the programmer can relate the output to the point where it was generated. The flexibility and selectivity of the snapshot maximize the amount of useful information which is obtained and minimize the amount of redundant data which surrounds it.

The problems of debugging are not entirely over when the source of an error has been located: the error still has to be corrected. The trouble is that, as has been noted earlier, the correction can itself be a source of additional errors unless care is taken. The offending code must only be altered when it is certain that it is the source of the error and that the alteration will cure the error. It is essential to check that the alteration will not have side effects and cause other problems, perhaps elsewhere in the program. This is particularly difficult when testing and debugging a program interactively at a terminal. The psychological pressure to act immediately and somehow to 'keep up with the computer' is stimulating, but it also tempts the programmer to make hasty and ill-considered decisions which can increase, rather than reduce, the number of errors in the program.

One further aspect of debugging remains to be mentioned: the fact that a working program may on occasion malfunction not through any fault of its own, but because of an external error. Examples of these are errors in a compiler or in system software, faults in the hardware, or mistakes by the operations staff. The novice programmer all too easily jumps to the conclusion that the machine must have made a mistake. One soon learns with experience that the incidence of machine errors is so small that, initially, it is reasonable to assume that the program is at fault. However, the possibility of some external error can never be completely discounted, and must be considered if an error is particularly recalcitrant.

Compilers, being large programs, cannot be expected to be totally error-free. However, except for very new compilers the bugs you are likely to encounter should be known and documented in your installation. Such errors are most likely to affect lesser-used features of the language, and can usually be avoided by treating them as language restrictions. Most system software errors can also be avoided, but in both cases, steps should be taken to rectify the faults if possible. They should certainly be noted and documented, as should the steps taken in the program to avoid them, and the reasons for those steps.

Both hardware and operator errors are characterized by being intermittent, or being related to some particular individual or piece of equipment. Good program design, using firewalling between modules, checksums, and batch totals on files, can be used to limit the damage caused by hardware errors, while programs which are sympathetic to their operators will be less prone to human errors. While it is practicable to ask the operator to enter parameters from the console when only one program is running in the machine, this can impose an unreasonable burden in a multiprogramming environment, with the consequent risk of mistakes. The solution lies in easier, more automatic programs with clear and concise operating instructions. The use of checkpoints, dumps, and restarts, which limit the processing lost by a hardware or operator error, is discussed in Section 4.4.

Program testing and debugging lacks the glamour of program design and building, and so is often ignored or only half done. It is tempting, after the white heat of coding, to assume that if the program compiles and runs without any execution errors, then it works. Perhaps it does work, but all it proves is that the program does something – not that it does the right thing. Only thorough testing can validate the program, and demonstrate that it does indeed meet its specification.

Nick Rushby

3.3 IMPROVING RUN-TIME PERFORMANCE

Let us assume that your project has now reached the stage where the program is developed, fully tested, and (as far as can be ascertained) error-free. Even if it fully meets its specification, there may still be the need for further modification, most notably to increase run-time efficiency in terms of either (or both of) execution time or store requirement. In this section we shall not be concerned with the special problems of programs which are too large when running in production to fit into the main store of the available system, or whose execution times are extremely long, though the techniques which are discussed here will naturally go some way towards dealing with such situations. However, even if the store requirement of your program can be met by the system, and the execution time is not so long that it causes operational problems, there may still be good reasons for improving efficiency. If you or your employer is being charged for the computer resources used, then execution time and quite possibly also store requirement will be major factors in the costs. Alternatively, if you are sharing a machine, even without explicit charging you may have to operate within some definite allocation of resources, and may well wish to maximize what can be done within that allocation. Even though there may be no specific limit on allocation, there may be benefits to be obtained from greater efficiency, such as a better turnround in a batch system, or a crisper response from an interactive system.

Choice and design of algorithm, choice of programming language, and the structure of the program will all play a significant part in the run-time performance of any program, and these of course are factors which must be borne in mind throughout. This section suggests useful methods of improving still further upon whatever good program design and construction may have done to make the program reasonably efficient in the first place – factors to look out for, techniques to try out.

Efficiency improvements

Let us start by considering some very basic rules that should be applied when writing programs designed to carry out numerical calculations, for example engineering applications, and then examine more complicated techniques to improve program efficiency.

The basic rules to remember are:

1. Arithmetic operations take approximately the following relative times on typical current computers:

    integer assignment $= 1$
    integer addition/subtraction $= 1.5$
    real assignment $= 2$
    real addition/subtraction $= 3$
    real multiplication $= 5$
    integer to real conversion $= 6$
    integer multiplication $= 8$
    division $= 9$
    exponentiation to integral power $= 35$
    exponentiation to real power $= 115$
    arithmetic functions (log, sqrt, sin) $= 150+$

Hence, for example, the following expressions on the left are best replaced by those on the right:

Original	Replace by
$2.0 * x$	$x + x$
$x/10.0$	$x * 0.1$
$x ** 2.0$	$x * x$

Such changes normally make no difference to the readability of the program.

2. An expression (or sequence of expressions) containing a repeated sub-expression should be broken up so that the sub-expression is evaluated only once, for example

    $$z = x * y + w/(x * y) ** 2.5$$

    can become

    $$xy = x * y$$
    $$z = xy + w/(xy ** 2.5)$$

Again it is usually possible to do this without harming the clarity of the program, though occasionally some additional comment is desirable.

One instance of repeated evaluation which is sometimes overlooked is the repeated call of a function with the same arguments. Where a function is going to be called repeatedly with a limited and predictable range of values of the arguments, it is worth considering evaluating these at the outset and storing the values in a table. In extreme cases improvements of the order of a factor of ten have been made by such methods!

3. Always remove constant expressions from within loops, and try to improve expressions that depend on loop control variables; for example replace the following Fortran code:

```
DO 10 I = 1, 25
    A(I) = X(I)/Z + SQRT(Y)
10   CONTINUE
```

by

```
P = SQRT(Y)
Q = 1.0/Z
DO 10 I = 1, 25
    A(I) = X(I)*Q + P
10   CONTINUE
```

(this rule of course applies equally well to loops in all kinds of programs, not just those for numerical applications).

However, as with the application of all rules, it is essential to keep a sense of proportion. It is terribly easy to go to the trouble of multiplying instead of dividing, or whatever, in a part of the program that is going to be performed once only per run, while failing to spot something appalling. It should be stressed that some rules, such as using $n + n$ instead of $2 * n$, are hardly worthwhile on many occasions, but it is simple to do and never does any harm. If you get into the habit, then you will automatically do it without needing special thought in the cases where it does matter. It is important, however, not to do it so thoughtlessly as to write something like $x(i+2,j)+x(i+2,j)$ instead of $2*x(i+2,j)$ because of the extra overheads incurred by array accesses.

Most numerical applications involve the manipulation of vectors and matrices of one sort or another, but, although an array is the ideal way to describe a matrix, the time taken to access a particular element can become embarrassing if you realize that at least one integer multiplication and two integer additions are conventionally required to select an element of a two-dimensional array, which incidentally is one of the most common data structures used by numerical applications programs. If we compare the relative times taken to multiply two matrices together using the following Fortran coded algorithms

```
SUBROUTINE AMULT(A, B, C, I, J, K)
DIMENSION A(I,J), B(J,K), C(I,K)
C INSERT CHECKS ON VALIDITY OF PARAMETERS HERE
DO 30 II = 1, I
    DO 20 IK = 1, K
        C(II,IK) = 0.0
        DO 10 IJ = 1, J
            C(II,IK) = C(II,IK) + A(II,IJ)*B(IJ,IK)
10           CONTINUE
```

```
20        CONTINUE
30     CONTINUE
       RETURN
       END



       SUBROUTINE BMULT(A, B, C, I, J, K)
       DIMENSION A(I,J), B(J,K), C(I,K)
C INSERT CHECKS ON VALIDITY OF PARAMETERS HERE
       DO 30 II = 1, I
         DO 20 IK = 1, K
         TERM = 0.0
         DO 10 IJ = 1, J
           TERM = TERM + A(II,IJ)*B(IJ,IK)
10         CONTINUE
         C(II,IK) = TERM
20       CONTINUE
30     CONTINUE
       RETURN
       END
```

we obtain the timings:

		AMULT	BMULT
A 3 * 3	B 3 * 1	2	1
	B 3 * 3	4	3
A 10 * 10	B 10 * 1	12	8
	B 10 * 10	105	74
A 50 * 50	B 50 * 1	2621	1820
	B 50 * 50	13319	9147

from which the benefits of the modified version should be obvious.

A second tip to remember is that the straightforward evaluation of a poly-
nomial can be advantageously improved. Compare the following algorithms, this
time coded in Algol 60, paying particular attention to the removal of the time-
consuming exponentiation:

   real procedure *apoly* (a, n, x);
      value n, x;
      real array a; **integer** n; **real** x ;
   comment in general, in Algol 60, it is most efficient to call scalar parameters by value unless they must be called by name. However, if an
   array is called by value it may be copied into local workspace, which
   is wasteful both of time and of space. In this case the protection of
   call by value is unnecessary;

```
begin real result;  integer count;
    result := a[0];
    for count := 1 step 1 until n
    do result := result + a [count] * x ↑ count;
    apoly := result
end apoly;
```

```
real procedure bpoly (b, n, x);
    value n, x;
    real array b;  integer n;  real x;
    comment as above. NOTE that the array a of constant values in
    apoly above is replaced here by the array b;
    begin real result;  integer count;
        result := b [n];
        for count := n − 1 step −1 until 0
        do result := result * x + b [count];
        bpoly := result
    end bpoly;
```

These examples show just how important the choice of algorithm can be − the 'efficiency' criterion discussed earlier in Section 1.3. The loop in *apoly* uses n exponentiations, n multiplications, and n additions (plus the overhead for incrementation of *count*); in *bpoly* the n exponentiations disappear, being absorbed into the other operations by the use of a superior algorithm.

Profilers

If, after your initial efficiency improvements, you still need to shorten your program's run-time, an extremely useful tool is a program execution profiler, already mentioned in the last section. As explained there, a profiler, in essence, produces a count of the number of times each program statement is executed during a particular run. While during program testing this is useful for detecting unexecuted statements, the primary use of a profiler is to determine where the major part of the execution of a program is taking place. It is those places, usually in the middle of loops, especially nested loops, that the maximum benefit can be obtained from an improvement in efficiency. Even the saving of one machine operation may be worthwhile if it is inside a loop which is executed hundreds or thousands of times. Development compilers often include a profiler as an aid to the programmer.

The importance of efficient coding, and the value of a profiler, are hammered home by the following example, admittedly an extreme case. This was the result of an experiment which the computer centre at University College London performed on a user's program with the aid of a profiler. When first examined, the program used 30 minutes of processor time and did not reach completion.

The profiler indicated that almost 80 percent of the time was spent in the loop

```
DO 6 J = 1, 1000
   IX(J) = IDAYS - IP(I)*J
   IF (IX(J) .LT. 0) GO TO 900
6    CONTINUE
900 IREM(I) = IP(I) + IX(J)
```

where all quantities are positive integers. As the sole aim of the loop was to find a remainder, it was replaced by

```
IREM(I) = MOD(IDAYS, IP(I))
```

and the execution time for completion dropped to seven and a half minutes. The program was then repeatedly reprofiled and further improved until the final version had an execution time of just over two and a half minutes.

Optimizers

If you are writing a program that will be heavily used, you should seriously consider the possibility of using an optimizing compiler to produce your final compiled version of the program. An optimizing compiler is one that uses special compilation techniques to produce faster object code for a given program than would be produced by a standard development compiler; a development compiler does not employ these techniques, because they can severely increase the compilation time of a particular program.

It is obviously not appropriate in this book to give a detailed explanation of the particular optimizations carried out by any one compiler; however, we can examine the basic techniques that are likely to be used by them all. In general, there are two basic machine independent optimizations that a compiler will perform: 'loop' optimizations and 'statement block' optimizations, where 'loop' has the programmer's normal meaning and 'statement block' is used to describe a series of statements uninterrupted in their flow of control (see Section 1.3). An optimizing compiler for a particular machine will also use techniques to exploit the hardware features of the machine, for example fast instructions to manipulate small constants, or to set a value to zero with a single instruction without using the arithmetic unit.

The first optimization made to loops is the obvious one of evaluating once only, outside the loop, all expressions whose value is unchanged on successive iterations of the loop. At this point a few words of warning are in order; some optimizing compilers will move out of the loop expressions which should not necessarily always be evaluated; for example

```
DO 10 I = 1, 5
   IF (N .NE. 0) A(I) = A(I)*10.0 / FLOAT(N)
10    CONTINUE
```

is quite likely to fail when the value of 10.0/FLOAT(N) is calculated before execution of the loop, if N actually has the value zero. In this case the programmer himself should have written, say

```
SCALE = 1.0
IF (N .NE. 0) SCALE = SCALE*10.0 / FLOAT(N)
```

or some equivalent outside the loop, and

```
A(I) = A(I)*SCALE
```

within it, but things are not always quite so obvious. Also, most optimizers assume, by default, that all functions referenced are normal; that is, they do not change their parameters, do not change global values, do not perform input/output or cause other program events, and repeated calls with the same parameters will deliver the same value. The other main optimization associated with loops involves the access of array elements whose subscripts are simply related to the loop control variable, when a technique known as linear incrementation, which dispenses with the normal overheads, can be used.

The first optimization made to a statement block is again an obvious choice. Any expression that occurs more than once and whose value is unchanged is evaluated only once, and similarly the calculations needed to select repeatedly a particular array element are performed only once; in this context, functions are again assumed to be normal by default. Because a statement block is compiled as a entity, the compiler remembers the current values stored in the registers of the target machine that it is compiling the program to run on, and can avoid the production of a certain amount of object code, in particular the needless reloading of a register with a value it already contains. A further optimization likely to be used for Fortran programs is the inline expansion of statement functions. Remember that we have mentioned only the most basic optimizations that a compiler can perform; there are many optimizers now in use that perform much more elaborate source code improvements and also analyse and improve the object code that they produce to use the full capabilities of the hardware.

Before you use an optimizing compiler you will, of course, have thoroughly tested the program, using an ordinary compiler as suggested in Section 3.2; but you should remember that the optimized program may not be executed in exactly the same way as the unoptimized version, both with respect to statement order and also order of evaluation of expressions, and that an optimizing compiler is often less forgiving in the language standards that it will accept. For these reasons it is just as essential that you retest the program after compiling it with an optimizer, as it is for any other change in the code.

We finish this description of optimizing compilers with a strong recommendation that you acquaint yourself with your particular compiler's capabilities, which will mean understanding the source optimizations it can perform (some compilers will produce a listing of the optimized source) and making yourself aware of the machine code optimizations likely to be used. Equally important, find out what are its weaknesses; for example, some optimizers do little to improve code partly optimized by hand, but do a good job on code written in a straightforward and simple-minded way.

Space improvements

We now turn to the question of economizing on the space requirements of a program. An optimizer may be able to help here to some extent, because it often condenses and compacts the actual machine code as well as increasing processing speed; but apart from this there are other techniques which the programmer can use to reduce the size of his program. Some machine-dependent techniques are discussed in Section 4.3, but here we discuss simple machine-independent ways to save space.

The obvious way to save space is to use only as much for data storage as is essential for the particular task. It is often possible to use temporary disk storage as work space and to hold intermediate results, although there are obvious time penalties associated with this technique.

Traditional data structures may be inappropriate for the problem, for example a sparse matrix is best stored in some form other than a straightforward array. Rather than spend a great deal of time trying to devise your own methods of doing this, once again you should go back to the literature for guidance, or seek advice. You will also find that some languages are much more suitable than others for implementation of such methods, and you will have to decide, if the language you are using is not convenient for such techniques, whether the effort required is worth the saving you will achieve.

A second way to economize on space is to share portions between data structures with disjoint life-times; this technique is natural for a block structured language, such as Algol 68, as the following example illustrates:

```
begin
    . . . . . . . . . .
    begin
        [1 : 1000] real temp 1;
        . . . . . . . . . .
        code using temp 1
        . . . . . . . . . .
    end;
    . . . . . . . . . .
    begin
        [1 : 1000] int temp 2;
        . . . . . . . . . .
        code using temp 2
        . . . . . . . . . .
    end;
    . . . . . . . . . .
end
```

However, such economies can often be implemented when using a language that supports only static data areas. The following example illustrates how to achieve the above effect in Fortran:

```
REAL TEMP1
INTEGER TEMP2
DIMENSION TEMP1(1000), TEMP2(1000)
EQUIVALENCE (TEMP1(1), TEMP2(1))
................
code using TEMP1
................
code using TEMP2
................
END
```

Care is necessary to ensure that the life-times of TEMP1 and TEMP2 are truly disjoint, but this technique is often used in large applications packages. PL/I is an example of a language that offers both the indirect techniques of block structuring and a variety of direct techniques for superposition of data areas and re-use of store.

Yet another way to achieve economy of data space usage is to employ dynamically adjusting data structures; this is a natural technique for a language that supports dynamic data storage, and again the Algol languages spring to mind, for example

```
begin
      int size of problem;
      read (size of problem);
      [1 : size of problem] real data;
      . . . . . . . . . .
end
```

It is often possible, by using system-dependent tricks, to obtain dynamic data structures in a language that nominally supports only static storage; an example using Fortran follows.

This uses the non-standard DIMENSION statement mentioned in Section 2.2, and requires GROW to be a system-dependent subroutine that can increase the size of the blank common area, and hence DATA. It also assumes that it is possible to suppress array-bound checking. It can even be possible for a Fortran program to use more than one variable sized array, using the above techniques and one extra trick:

```
      INTEGER SIZE1, SIZE2
      DIMENSION WORK(1)
      COMMON WORK
      READ (5,5) SIZE1, SIZE2
    5 FORMAT (2I6)
      CALL GROW(SIZE1 + SIZE2)
      CALL MAIN(WORK, SIZE1, WORK(SIZE1 + 1), SIZE2)
      END
      SUBROUTINE MAIN(DATA1, SIZE1, DATA2, SIZE2)
C THIS IS THE MAIN CONTROL ROUTINE OF THE PROGRAM
      INTEGER SIZE1, SIZE2
      DIMENSION DATA1(SIZE1), DATA2(SIZE2)
      . . . . . . . . . . . . . . . . .
      END
```

The extra trick (surprisingly, allowed by the standard) is to pass an array element to MAIN, instead of an array, for the second array parameter.

The benefits of efficient store requirements that are gained by using dynamic allocation techniques can be very great if the sizes of problem that a program is meant to handle cover a wide range; however, you will need to remember how the size varies from problem to problem in order to estimate the size of the program for any particular run.

Let us now turn our attention to some considerations to bear in mind in relation to recursion and data space. An algorithm that uses recursion should be used only if the problem's data structures are naturally recursive (see Section 1.3); this on its own, however, is not sufficient reason to use a recursive technique. To use recursion effectively requires at least 2 recursive calls, for example the following recursive search of a linear list, this time written in Pascal:

```
TYPE INFO = - - - - - - ;
    LIST = ↑ LISTELEMENT;
    LISTELEMENT = RECORD (VALUE: INFO;
                          NEXT: LIST);

FUNCTION SEARCHLIST(L: LIST): LIST;
    VAR RESULT: LIST;
BEGIN
    IF - - - - - - THEN
        RESULT := - - - - - -
    ELSE IF L↑.NEXT <> NIL THEN
        RESULT := SEARCHLIST(L↑.NEXT)
    ELSE RESULT := NIL;
    SEARCHLIST := RESULT;
END;
```

gains nothing over

```
FUNCTION SEARCHLIST(L: LIST): LIST;
    VAR FOUND: BOOLEAN;
BEGIN
    FOUND := FALSE;
    SEARCHLIST := NIL;
    REPEAT
        IF - - - - - - THEN BEGIN
            FOUND := TRUE;
            SEARCHLIST := L
        END ELSE L := L↑.NEXT
    UNTIL (L = NIL) OR FOUND
END;
```

and will be necessarily slower and use more space. However, searching a binary tree recursively is natural because there is no redundant information passed from one call to the next.

Just as with dynamic data space allocation mentioned earlier, recursive algorithms use a varying amount of storage depending on the attributes of a particular problem; but this time it is often more difficult to predict the space needed. There are also some recursive algorithms that are inapplicable in particular cases.

We conclude these thoughts on space improvements by briefly considering some different ways to store character strings. If you have a free hand in selecting the language to use for an application that handles characters and text, then you would be wise to choose one that supports the necessary data types (character and string) properly; the languages that spring to mind immediately are Snobol and Algol 68, as mentioned in Section 2.1. However, you may be constrained to use a less suitable language, such as Fortran (pre-Fortran 77, which does contain some character handling facilities). Although most implementations have methods (usually primitive) of storing and manipulating fixed amounts of textual information, you may well have to provide your own method of economically storing variable-length strings of characters. If you are handling a number of strings, you will need some kind of rudimentary store management system, for example a large array, to hold the text in whatever form your implementation conveniently allows, and other arrays to record the starting positions and lengths of the strings. Considering the problems which arise when one string has to be increased in length, the complications can be imagined, compared with what happens with languages that perform all these chores automatically. The book by A. C. Day listed in the bibliography is recommended as a source of good ideas for those placed in this situation.

On the other hand, simply because a language does support such facilities as variable-length strings does not mean that you can forget all your worries! Such facilities do not come free of charge (in the sense of time and space) and if you are trying to make your program efficient and economic of space it is up to you to find out what the overheads are in using a particular facility. In this subsection we have mentioned only the simplest data structures, arrays and strings, but this argument applies with even more force to the more complex data structures ('records') allowed in languages like Cobol, PL/I, Pascal, and Algol 68.

System considerations

Everthing so far has been discussed on the assumption that the program is to be run by a single conventional sequential processor and with a specific allocation of store which it may (for example in a multi-programming batch system) be desirable to minimize. However, other forms of computer architecture and operating system environment are possible, and are becoming increasingly important, introducing further factors which need to be taken into account if relevant, even if the language used and the program text remain the same. Space precludes an exhaustive discussion of all the possibilities, which in any case mostly at present affect only a small proportion of installations. The one which does, however, apply to a significant number of installations already, and is likely to increase greatly, is that of 'paging' or 'virtual memory' systems. Although the idea of such systems is that the programmer can behave as if he has unlimited main store available, and hence does not have to worry about some of the problems discussed in the next chapter, again not all his worries are over, for he is not getting 'something for nothing'.

The price to be paid for a virtual memory system is that, every time a page has to be swapped between backing store and main store, a system overhead is incurred, noticeable to the programmer in increased run-times, and perhaps also in costs. The phenomenon to try to avoid when using any virtual memory system is that of 'thrashing', where repeatedly, typically in a loop, pages are referenced which are not currently resident in main store. It is sufficient to illustrate this in the obvious case of major importance, that of array access.

Assume that a real value can be stored in one machine word and that a page in virtual memory is 1024 words. Then the following two fragments of Fortran achieve the same effect, but take very different times to do so:

```
DIMENSION A(1024,100)
DO 20 I = 1, 1024
    DO 10 J = 1, 100
        A(I,J) = 0.0
10      CONTINUE
20  CONTINUE
```

```
      DIMENSION A(1024,100)
      DO 20 J = 1, 100
        DO 10 I = 1, 1024
          A(I,J) = 0.0
10      CONTINUE
20    CONTINUE
```

Remembering that a Fortran array is stored in such a way that the first subscript varies most rapidly (that is $A(1, 1)$, $A(2, 1)$, ... $A(1024, 1)$, $A(1, 2)$, ... in the above examples), we see that in the first case each cycle of the loop involves a different page of virtual memory from the previous one, resulting in a high system overhead. In the second case, the pages are accessed in a much more sedate and orderly fashion, and the system overhead is negligible in comparison. An interesting point about the above rearrangements is that some optimizing compilers cannot properly optimize the first example, whereas they can manage to speed up the second. In general, it is the programmer's responsibility when using a virtual memory system to be aware of how his program and data are organized into pages, and to take this into account if system overheads appear to be significant.

Modern hardware design offers many more facilities, especially to speed up the execution time (both processor time and real elapsed time) taken by a program. Pipelines, slaves, and microcoded functions are now being used to accelerate sequential execution, the last affecting the typical times quoted at the beginning of this section, if such things as mathematical functions are computed by hardware rather than software. Parallel processing is being used so that different parts of a computation can be carried out simultaneously by different processors. This possibility can affect algorithm design, and facilities offered as extensions or library routines for conventional languages. Nevertheless, optimizers may be able to exploit such facilities in ordinary languages, for example by evaluating the two products in

$$X*X + Y*Y$$

simultaneously in different processors, or (with more difficulty) by reordering (and assigning to different processors) parts of a simple (non-branching or non-looping) sequence of program statements. Again the programmer needs to be aware of the possibilities, and the consequences of writing a piece of code in a given way. Probably the most significant sort of parallel processing, however, is array processing, where the same operation can be carried out simultaneously on all the elements of an array (up to some maximum size) by an 'array processor', effectively an array of processing units under a single overall controller. This again has implications for algorithm design and the way programs are written.

In short, to get the best out of your system, find out what it can do and —
just as important — what it cannot do, or does not do very well; and tune your
program accordingly. There are two provisos, however: the more you do this,
the more the program will be system-dependent and hence difficult to transport
and vulnerable to system changes; and, there may come a time when the improvements you are making do not justify the human effort and machine resources
which the extra development and testing demand. Keep a sense of proportion!

John Steel

CHAPTER 4

Special Problems

The five sections of this chapter deal in general terms with certain important classes of problems which can arise in various situations. The first section discusses what happens if a problem has no known feasible algorithmic solution, and hence some heuristic strategy is needed. The second and third sections are concerned with coping with the problems which arise when the data to be handled by a program, or the program itself, becomes too large for the available store. The fourth section discusses the problems of programs which have very long or indefinite run times, and the fifth the particular problems of programming for real-time systems which have to deal with external events, such as those for monitoring or control of industrial processes. The second and third sections overlap somewhat with each other and with the final section of the last chapter, Section 3.3; otherwise, except for the fact that many real-time process control programs have to run for long periods, the various sections are largely independent and may be read in any order, or omitted at a first reading.

4.1 HEURISTIC PROGRAMMING

Many of the more interesting and difficult programming tasks involve using a computer to solve problems posed in the form 'Is there a way to. . . . . .? What is the shortest path to. . . . . . .? List all possible. . . . Is there an arrangement of these things that satisfies. . . . . .?'

Characteristic of such problems is that they potentially involve an exhaustive search of all possible arrangements of some finite set. If uncontrolled, this exhaustive search can lead to what has been called the 'combinatorial explosion' — an exponential increase in the size of search with problem dimension. Heuristic programming has come to mean the use of domain-specific knowledge to damp down this explosion of possibilities by guiding the search in promising directions first. This problem-dependent feature of the technique means that almost by definition one can give only examples rather than generalities.

However, experience shows that the difficulty most people have with this kind of programming is not so much in tuning the heuristic part to the peak of efficiency, but rather in knowing how to start at all; and so the aim of this section is to present a general framework into which the domain-specific heuristic can be fitted in as structural and modular a way as possible.

Consider the well-known knight's tour problem on a conventional chessboard. The task is to start with the knight on a given square, say the corner one, and to visit every other square on the board just once. How many ways are there to do it? Does the size of board matter? Is it even possible?

Asked to describe a methodical way of tackling it you would probably say something like 'From the square the knight is currently on go to any square not previously visited and start again at the beginning of this sentence. If no square is available from the current square go back to the square you got to it from and start again at the beginning of the previous sentence'. Refining this and formalizing it a bit more (cf the section on structured programming, Section 2.4) we assume that the solution to the problem consists of a vector $x_1, x_2, \ldots \ldots$ satisfying certain constraints, each x_i being a member of some set X_i. In the case of the knight's tour the x_i are the names of squares, the constraints are that no two are the same and the coordinates of x_{i-1} and x_i obey the knight's move rule, the X_i being the currently unvisited squares. One method of exhaustive search would consider as potential solutions all members of the set $X_1 \times X_2 \ldots \ldots \times X_{64}$,

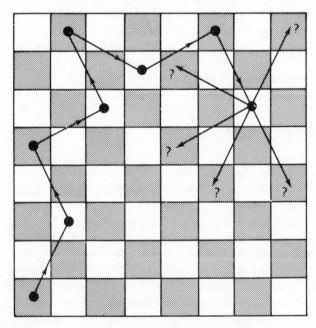

Fig. 4.1A – The knight's tour problem.

64! in all, checking each to see if the constraints were satisfied. Clearly this is computationally unfeasible, and yet equally clearly every possible solution must somehow be considered before we can be sure how many there are, if any.

In the next part we introduce a general framework for carrying out exhaustive searches such as this within which heuristics for the efficient solution of particular problems can be fitted in a reasonably modular way.

The backtracking algorithm

Suppose we have a partial solution $[x_1, x_2, \ldots\ldots, x_k]$ that satisfies the constraints, and that Y_{k+1} is the subset of X_{k+1} representing feasible (constraint-satisfying) possibilities for x_{k+1}, in our example the squares reachable by the knight from x_k that have not been visited previously. Then the two sentences in quotation marks above translate into 'let x_{k+1} be the next member of Y_{k+1} not previously considered, then the new partial solution is $[x_1, \ldots\ldots x_{k+1} \ldots\ldots]$ and now generate Y_{k+2}, but if you cannot find an x_{k+1} because all members of Y_{k+1} have been considered, scrap the current x_k as a candidate and replace it by the next member of Y_k'. Putting this into Algol-like language we get:

$Y_1 \leftarrow X_1$ [the set of all possibilities for x_1]
$k \leftarrow 1$

while $k > 0$ **do** $\left\{\begin{array}{l} \textbf{while } Y_k \textbf{ not empty do} \\ \\ \\ \text{[backtrack] } k \leftarrow k-1; \end{array}\right.$ $\left\{\begin{array}{l} \text{[go forward]} \\ x_k \leftarrow \text{next from } Y_k; \\ Y_k \leftarrow Y_k - x_k; \\ \textbf{if}(x_1 \ldots x_k) \text{ is a solution} \\ \qquad\qquad\qquad \textbf{then} \\ \text{do something with it;} \\ k \leftarrow k+1; \\ \text{compute } Y_k \end{array}\right.$

This is naturally recursive, and equivalently we can write:

procedure *backtrack* (x,i); [x is the partial solution vector]
if x is a solution **then** do something with it;
compute Y_i;
for all y in Y_i **do** *backtrack* $(x|y, i+1)$;
return

called by setting x to the null vector and invoking *backtrack* $(x,1)$, the actual backtracking being hidden by the recursion mechanism.

For those condemned to the logical spaghetti of Fortran-like languages the equivalent might be:

```
   K = 1
   set Y(1) as a pointer to the head of a list of possibilities for X(1
10 IF (Y(K) is null) GO TO 11
   X(K) = the element pointed to by Y(K)
   Y(K) is incremented
   IF (the vector X is a solution) do something like printing it
   K = K + 1
   set Y(K) as a pointer to the list of possibilities for X(K)
   GO TO 10
11 K = K - 1
   IF (K .GT. 0) GO TO 10
   STOP
```

In many cases, of course, Y(K) is present only by implication, the set of possibilities for X(K) being generated as required or indexed incrementally as in generating permutations in lexicographic order. Also solutions are often of fixed length (for example, 64 for the knight's tour) and a test can be inserted after incrementing K to jump if the limit is violated to the backtrack at label 11. This is about as far as one can go in complete generality, and we conclude this part with an illustration of how the domain-specific components slot into this framework by returning to the knight's tour, and showing how the last pseudo-Fortran program could be successively refined to tackle the problem.

```
      LOGICAL VIS(64)
      INTEGER NSQ(64), MV(64), MOVES(64,8)
      K = 1
      set array VIS to .FALSE. except VIS(starting square) = .TRUE.
      NSQ(1) = starting square
      GO TO 11
   10 MV(K) = MV(K) + 1
      IF (MV(K) .GT. 8) GO TO 13
      I = MOVES(K, MV(K))
      IF (VIS(I) .OR. position I is off the board) GO TO 10
      NSQ(K) = I
      VIS(I) = .TRUE.
      IF (K .EQ. 64) GO TO 12
C     go forward
   11 K = K + 1
      MV(K) = 0
      CALL MOVGEN(MOVES, NSQ, K)
      GO TO 10
   12 solution found (in NSQ) so do something with it
C     backtrack
   13 VIS(NSQ(K)) = .FALSE.
      K = K - 1
      IF (K .GT. 1) GO TO 10
      STOP
```

This is fairly self-explanatory, the logical array VIS keeping track of the squares visited and the partial solution being stored in NSQ, while MV records the next move to be tried at depth K. MOVGEN is a subroutine that implements the knight's move to store in MOVES the squares currently available at depth K. It is not of course necessary to store these explicitly, and indeed there are some particularly efficient ways of generating and testing chess moves for legality, but to explain these here would involve going into too much detail.

As yet this program contains no heuristics, and indeed if run as it stands on anything more sluggish than a Cray 1 it would produce very little in the way of observable results even for the 8×8 board. The best way to see what is happening during execution of a backtracking algorithm is to consider the process as generating a tree structure that traces the history of the computation.

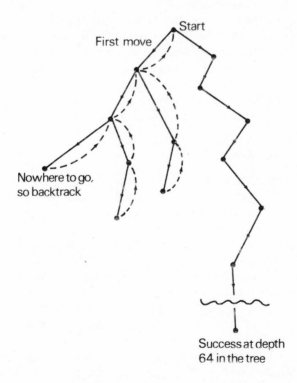

Fig. 4.1B – Tree of the progress of the knight's tour computation.

Clearly the behaviour of the knight's tour program is completely determined by the order in which the moves are considered, and this is fixed by what happens in subroutine MOVGEN, which is therefore the place where the heuristics must be put.

At first sight it might appear that a good strategy would be to move to squares that keep a lot of options open: that is, from which there are as many unvisited squares as possible available. But this is in fact disastrous, and a look at the tree will show why. The tendency would then be to put off meeting dead-ends as long as possible, whereas a more effective plan is to prove as soon as you can that a path gets nowhere, or in the customary horticultural metaphor, to prune as near to the root as possible.

In the knight's tour this can be achieved by completely the opposite strategy of choosing to move first to squares with as few exits as possible, and if implemented this one heuristic enables even larger tours than the 8×8 to be found quite quickly. In terms of the specimen program the relevant test is put into MOVGEN in the obvious way, no other alteration to the structure being required.

The tree metaphor is important in such cases because it provides a model of what is happening, and indeed can be used as the basis for a mathematical analysis of many problems. It must not be confused with the data structures that are used by the program; no tree is actually stored, indeed it is evident that backtracking, in its simplest form, uses no more than a pushdown stack.

We conclude this part by considering briefly a commonly occurring class of problems where early pruning of the tree is similarly effective.

Minimum-cost solutions

In many applications it is known that there are several solutions, but that a cost can be attached to each, and what is required is the solution of minimum overall cost. Typical of this type is the travelling salesman problem where the gentleman concerned has to visit a number of customers and return to his starting point, incurring in general a cost A_{ij} in going from i to j. In what order should he visit his customers to minimize the cost of his round trip? Note that this is a different kind of problem from the knight's tour; there it was not obvious that a solution existed at all, here there are clearly $n!$ possible journeys if there are n customers, and the point at issue is whether the optimal one can be found without generating all of them. It turns out that backtracking again provides the appropriate framework within which to hang the heuristics that make efficient solutions possible. In fact a well-known algorithm called 'branch-and-bound' is really just backtracking with the obvious heuristic that, if the cost of a partial solution exceeds that of the best complete solution so far, then that partial solution is not worth developing any further. (Note that for this to be sound the cost functions must satisfy the relation $cost(x_1 \ldots x_k) \leqslant cost(x_1 \ldots x_{k+1})$). Assuming this to be so, that algorithm would be:

mincost←∞; *partcost*←0; Y_1←X_1; k←1;
while k>0 **do begin while** Y_k not null **and** *partcost* < *mincost* **do**
      begin
      x_k← next from Y_k;Y_k←Y_k less x_k;
      partcost←*cost*(x_1.....x_k);
      if (x_1.....x_k) is a solution **and** *partcost* <*mincost*
      then *save*(x_1.......x_k) and set *mincost*←*partcost*;
      k←k+1; compute Y_k
      end;
    k←k-1; *partcost*←*cost*(x_1.....x_k)
    end

the minimum cost solution being that last recorded by the procedure *save*.

It is instructive to apply this type of algorithm to a small travelling salesman problem, printing out the search tree that was mentioned earlier as tracing the path taken by the program in execution. It will be found that this partial-solution-cost heuristic ('theorem' really, because it can be proved completely sound) does eliminate part of the search tree, but that the effect is rather weak, and deep penetration can occur before branches are pruned. If customers 1 and 2 are far apart, then tours beginning 1, 2 are going to waste a lot of time, and in general it is clear that near-optimal solutions should be found as soon as possible by rearranging the tree to make this likely. Some very sophisticated heuristics have been developed for doing this dynamically, and those interested are referred to the bibliography for the details.

We go on to consider a generalization of backtracking and a special type of heuristic that is useful in many problem-solving programs.

Graph searching with an evaluation function

Many non-numerical programming tasks can be described in terms of starting with a set of initial conditions and looking for a sequence of transformations that achieves some final desired state or goal. Examples are theorem-proving in mathematics where, given the axioms and rules of inference, the task would be to prove a specified theorem; or the construction of plans for robots where the goal might be to achieve a specified arrangement of objects within the robot's restricted world model.

Fundamental to all such problems is the state-space, the set of all possible problem descriptions, and the operators that can be applied to each, representing legal transformations from one state to another. Formally each state can be thought of as corresponding to a node in a graph and the operators as generating the edges. A search procedure traverses a subset of the whole state-space (the smaller the better, since this will be more efficient) to find a path from the initially specified state (start node) to one or more goal nodes.

A simple example that has been the subject of many experiments is quoted in the book by Nilsson (1971), incidentally a good basic reference on what was

known up to that date. This sliding block type of puzzle has n^2-1 square blocks
that can be moved within the constraints of an $n \times n$ array. The smallest nontrivial
version is the 8-puzzle, the problem being, starting with a given configuration, to
find a sequence of moves, sliding blocks into the vacant space, that leads to a
previously defined regular arrangement as the goal. (See Fig. 4.1C). Since any
move takes an even (or odd) permutation of the digits 1–8 into another even
(or odd) permutation, only half of the possible 9! configurations are accessible
in any given puzzle. The complete state-space then consists of all nodes corresponding to the 9!/2 possible configurations, and the transition operator is the procedure
that determines which moves can legally be made for each of these. A typical
problem and solution might be as shown in Fig. 4.1D.

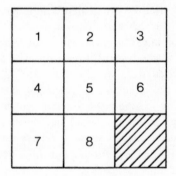

Fig. 4.1C – The 3 × 3 sliding block puzzle.

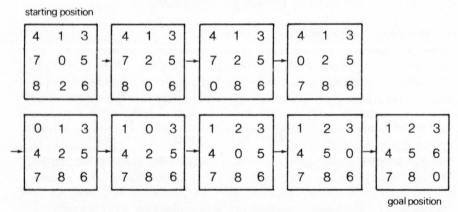

Fig. 4.1D – A possible 3 × 3 sliding block problem and solution. (0 = the vacant
space.)

In this graph-searching context, heuristic information, if available, can be
used to guide the search towards the goal by ensuring that nodes which lie on or
near a short solution path are generated first. However, before describing a general

algorithm for doing this we first specify two simple but essentially 'blind' procedures. Characteristic of the methods we consider in this section is the use of two lists, one of which contains nodes whose successors we have not yet explored, the other containing nodes whose successors have already been generated. Following Nilsson (1971) we call the first of these OPEN and the second CLOSED. The two simple algorithms then have the same structure specified by the following sequence of steps:

0) Put the start node on the OPEN list.
1) If OPEN is empty signal failure, else continue.
2) Take the first node, P say, off the OPEN list and put it on CLOSED.
3) Generate all successors of P [if none go to (2)] and put them at the beginning/end of OPEN [providing pointers back to P].
4) If any of these successors are goal nodes exit and trace back through the pointers for the solution, else go to (2).

The alternatives in Step 3 of putting the most recently generated nodes at the beginning and end of the OPEN list characterize, respectively, depth-first and breadth-first search procedures. Note that in the depth-first procedure the OPEN list is essentially a pushdown stack, and the algorithm is formally identical to that for backtracking that we considered above.

The breadth-first procedure is guaranteed to find an optimal (shortest-path) solution, but at the expense of possibly having to store a large number of intermediate configurations (which in practice may preclude finding a solution at all if it runs out of store). The definition of these two procedures seems to imply that they are at opposite ends of a continuum of possibilities and leads us to wonder what advantage could be gained by ordering nodes on the OPEN list in a more flexible way.

The ordered search algorithm

Suppose $f(x)$ to be a numerical function of node x, then the previous algorithm can be generalised as follows:

0) Put start node s on the OPEN list and compute $f(s)$.
1) If OPEN is empty signal failure, else continue.
2) Take off the OPEN list that node x for which $f(x)$ is the smallest and put it on CLOSED.
3) If x is a goal node exit with the solution obtained by tracing back through the pointers.
4) Generate all successors x_i of x and compute $f(x_i)$.
5) Add every x_i not on OPEN or CLOSED already to OPEN.
    For those already on OPEN change the stored $f(x_i)$ if the new value is smaller. For those already CLOSED if the new $f(x_i)$ is smaller than the stored value put x_i back on OPEN. If the $f(x_i)$ is changed redirect the pointers to x.
6) Goto (2).

It can be proved (see the Nilsson book) that if $f(x) = g(x)+h(x)$, where $g(x)$ is the distance from the start node to node x and $h(x)$ is a *lower bound* on the distance from x to a goal node, this ordered search algorithm is then guaranteed to find an optimal goal path if one exists.

To illustrate, return briefly to the 8-puzzle and take $h(x)$ as the number of misplaced blocks, taking the value 3 for the configuration

1	0	3
4	2	5
7	8	6

Clearly this is always a conservative estimate for the number of moves required to reach the goal (although in fact correct in this case).

The extreme cases of $h(x)$ identically zero and $h(x)$ always equal to the optimal goal path distance correspond respectively to breadth-first search, which may generate a large number of nodes before finding the guaranteed optimal path, and a perfect search which generates no redundant states. The continuum of possibilities in between results in searches that are variously efficient; generally speaking the more elaborate an estimate $h(x)$ is, and the closer to the true value, the more efficient the search, but the time taken to compute $h(x)$ must be taken into account, and in many cases ingenious but elaborate evaluation functions are rewarded by diminishing returns.

AND/OR graphs and game trees

The next step in the direction of increasing generalization lies in considering the case where problem states are not transformed into alternatives in a one-to-one way, but break down into subproblems *all* of which have to be solved before the original problem can be considered soluble.

In diagrammatic form P can be transformed into R or S or T of which R can be transformed to R_1 and R_2, S to S_1, and T to T_1, T_2 and T_3. (See Fig. 4.1E).

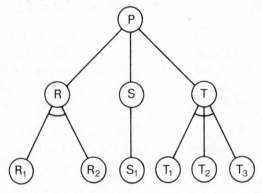

Fig. 4.1E

Nodes at which branching occurs into subproblems *all* of which must be solved are called AND nodes; they are denoted in the diagram by an arc connecting the subproblem edges. The other nodes at which problems transform one-to-one are OR nodes. The ordered search algorithm considered above operated on graphs all of whose nodes were OR nodes. For AND/OR graphs there are similar methods available based on heuristic functions involving cost, solubility, and path length.

Two-person games such as chess give rise to a special case of the AND/OR graph where the AND and OR nodes occur at alternate levels in the tree of possibilities from a given position. This is obvious from elementary considerations since, for example, if White is to force a win he must find *one* move (White to move is an OR node) which wins for *all* Black's replies (the AND node). Normally terminal (win, draw or lose) nodes are beyond the reach of a search, and numerical evaluation functions are used, leading to the well-known depth-first minimax procedure and its important refinement, the alpha-beta algorithm. Tree-searching in this context has been deeply studied as have AND/OR graphs in general. The refinements are beyond the scope of this section, the possibilities being mentioned here for the sake of completeness. Those interested are referred in the first case to Nilsson and then to the more recent and specialized literature.

Conclusion

We have specified two quite general methods, backtracking and the ordered-search algorithm, within which heuristics for the efficient solution of particular problems can be fitted in a modular and well-structured way. Quite deliberately we have concentrated on the outer shell of such programs rather than showing in detail what goes into the world's best chess program, because a structured approach is particularly important for heuristic programs, which tend to be complicated and hard to debug, and to need a lot of fine tuning.

Michael Clarke

4.2 LARGE QUANTITIES OF DATA

In this section we look at the problems caused when the quantity of data to be processed, rather than the program itself, is too large to fit into the available store. The problems are somewhat akin to, but by no means identical to, those which occur with very large programs. In cases where both the program and the data are very large, it will obviously be necessary to adopt some suitable combination of the techniques discussed in this section and the next.

The first thing to do, when it is found that the data is too much to fit into the store, is to look at the algorithm for its processing. As we shall see, it is likely that the algorithm will have to be changed anyway, but it is possible that a completely different choice of algorithm will eliminate the problem altogether. To take a very simple example, beginners on a programming course are commonly asked to write a program to find the mean and standard deviation of set of numbers. Very often, they do this by reading all the numbers into an array, and then processing the array to find the statistics required. Obviously, if the set of numbers is too large the array will be bigger than the available store. Yet the array is unnecessary (although this example is often given to introduce the techniques of array handling). The mean can be found by reading in the values one by one and accumulating a running total and a count of the number of items input. The basic definition of the standard deviation requires this mean, so an algorithm based on this definition requires the set of numbers to be scanned again, that is, either re-input, or stored in an array — as beginners sometimes point out when challenged to rewrite their program without using an array. However, the formula for the standard deviation can be reorganized in such a way that all that it is necessary to do is to read in the numbers one by one and accumulate, as well as the count and the running total, a further running total containing the sum of the squares of the individual items. From these three values the standard deviation can be calculated without any need for an array, however large the set may be. (However, the method may have disadvantages in other directions! The details are shown in Fig. 4.2A).

(a) Straightforward algorithm

Given a data set x_i $(i = 1, \ldots, n)$:

$$\text{Mean} = \left(\sum_{i=1}^{n} x_i \right) / n$$

$$\text{Standard deviation} = \sqrt{\left(\sum_{i=1}^{n} (x_i - mean)^2 \right) / n}$$

Essentials of coding (in Fortran)

```
      READ (5,100) (X(I), I = 1, N)
      SUM = 0.0
      DO 10 I = 1, N
        SUM = SUM + X(I)
10    CONTINUE
      XMEAN = SUM / FLOAT(N)
      SUMSQD = 0.0
      DO 20 I = 1, N
        DIFF = X(I) - XMEAN
        SUMSQD = SUMSQD + DIFF*DIFF
20    CONTINUE
      XSTDEV = SQRT(SUMSQD / FLOAT(N))
```

(b) Revised algorithm

This results from rewriting

$$\text{Standard deviation} = \sqrt{\left(\sum_{i=1}^{n} (x_i - mean)^2 \right)/n}$$

$$= \sqrt{\sum_{i=1}^{n} \left((x_i^2 - 2x_i\, mean + mean^2) \right)/n}$$

$$= \sqrt{\sum_{i=1}^{n} x_i^2 /n - 2 \times mean \times \left(\sum_{i=1}^{n} x_i \right)/n + mean^2}$$

$$= \sqrt{\left(\sum_{i=1}^{n} x_i^2 \right)/n - mean^2}$$

$$\text{since} \left(\sum_{i=1}^{n} x_1 \right)/n = mean$$

Essentials of coding:

```
     SUM = 0.0
     SUMSQ = 0.0
     DO 30 I = 1, N
        READ (5,300) XI
        SUM = SUM + XI
        SUMSQ = SUMSQ + XI*XI
30   CONTINUE
     XMEAN = SUM / FLOAT(N)
     XSTDEV = SQRT(SUMSQ / FLOAT(N) - XMEAN*XMEAN)
```

Important warning note: It will be seen that the algorithm depends on the calculation and then subtraction of two quantities derived from the totals SUM and SUMSQ. If the data set values (and hence the mean) are large compared with the standard deviation, XSTDEV will be calculated by the subtraction of two large quantities leaving a small quantity; that is, there is great danger that most of the significant figures will disappear leaving a 'result' which is mostly or wholly composed of rounding error! This shows once again that *all* aspects of a problem *must* be considered together, not in isolation — a device to save space may here ruin the results. This particular problem can be overcome by putting $y_i = x_i - x'$ where x' is a 'typical' x-value (it is often safe to take the first value x_1) and accumulating the sums of the x_i, the y_i and y_i^2. Mathematicians will be able to work out the new formula for the standard deviation, which still involves the subtraction of two values; but the values cannot now be very large compared to their difference, so the significant figures are not lost.

Fig. 4.2A – Mean and standard deviation.

It is worth staying with this example for a moment, despite its triviality. Suppose that, in addition, it is necessary to find the correlation between this set of numbers, and another set. The straightforward algorithm requires two arrays, one for each set. If the store will hold one such array but not both, it is perfectly possible to reorganize the algorithm to store the first set in an array, but then deal with the second set one item at a time, accumulating the necessary running totals to calculate the correlation at the end. If the store is not sufficient to hold even one set, however, other factors come into consideration. If the data is not captive (see Section 2.3), it will probably be possible to arrange for it to be input alternately from one set and the other, that is, in order a_1, b_1, a_2, b_2, a_3, ... etc. instead of a_1, a_2, a_3, ..., a_n, b_1, b_2, ... In this case again, the necessary running totals can be kept without the need for an array at all; the details are shown in Fig. 4.2B. If the data is, on the other hand, kept sequentially in two separate sets, much depends on whether a program can use two different input channels simultaneously, and whether the two sets can be made available on these channels. The point here is that it is not just the algorithm, but other factors such as the system configuration and the nature of the data, which have to be taken into account.

(a) Straightforward algorithm

Given data sets x_i, y_i $(i = 1, ..., n)$

$$\text{Correlation coefficient} = \frac{\sum_{i=1}^{n} (x_i - \bar{x})(y_i - \bar{y})}{\left[\sum_{i=1}^{n} (x_i - \bar{x})^2 \sum_{i=1}^{n} (y_i - \bar{y})^2 \right]^{\frac{1}{2}}}$$

Essentials of coding (in Fortran).

```
     READ (5,100) (X(I), I = 1, N), (Y(I), I = 1, N)
     XSUM = 0.0
     YSUM = 0.0
     DO 10 I = 1, N
       XSUM = XSUM + X(I)
       YSUM = YSUM + Y(I)
10   CONTINUE
     XMEAN = XSUM / FLOAT(N)
     YMEAN = YSUM / FLOAT(N)
     SMXSQD = 0.0
     SMYSQD = 0.0
     SUMXYD = 0.0
```

```
DO 20 I = 1, N
  XDIFF = X(I) - XMEAN
  YDIFF = Y(I) - YMEAN
  SMXSQD = SMXSQD + XDIFF*XDIFF
  SMYSQD = SMYSQD + YDIFF*YDIFF
  SUMXYD = SUMXYD + XDIFF*YDIFF
20   CONTINUE
  CORRXY = SUMXYD / SQRT(SMXSQD*SMYSQD)
```

(b) Revised algorithm

Similarly to the example in Fig. 4.2A, the correlation coefficient can be rewritten as

$$
\frac{\sum_{i=1}^{n} x_i y_i - (\sum_{i=1}^{n} x_i)(\sum_{i=1}^{n} y_i)/n}{\left[\sum_{i=1}^{n} x_i^2 - (\sum_{i=1}^{n} x_i)^2/n\right]\left[\sum_{i=1}^{n} y_i^2 - (\sum_{i=1}^{n} y_i)^2/n\right]^{1/2}}
$$

Essentials of coding:

```
XSUM = 0.0
YSUM = 0.0
XSUMSQ = 0.0
YSUMSQ = 0.0
XYSUM = 0.0
DO 30 I = 1, N
  READ (5,300) XI, YI
  XSUM = XSUM + XI
  YSUM = YSUM + YI
  XSUMSQ = XSUMSQ + XI*XI
  YSUMSQ = YSUMSQ + YI*YI
  XYSUM = XYSUM + XI*YI
30   CONTINUE
  CORRXY = (XYSUM - XSUM*YSUM / FLOAT(N))
1        / SQRT(   (XSUMSQ - XSUM*YSUM / FLOAT(N))
2                * (YSUMSQ - YSUM*YSUM / FLOAT(N)) )
```

Important note: Similar warnings apply as in Fig. 4.2A.

Fig. 4.2B – Correlation coefficient.

If a simple change of algorithm does not solve the problem, at least on its own, the next thing to look at is the kind of data structure being used. The correlation example shows how the order of processing of data items can affect the store requirement, but now we are concerned rather with the way the data is stored. Let us take another simple example to illustrate the kind of points that can arise. Quite commonly, arrays are used to code information, for example in a market research survey various arrays may be used to store encoded responses which must analysed and correlated, the array index referring to an individual respondent. Some of these arrays may be largely empty of information in the sense that most respondents will give the same response. In such cases it may be possible instead to keep an array of the indices of those who gave a non-standard response, plus a record of what that response was if more than one non-standard response is possible. Different data structures might be considered, such as linear linked lists if processing is sequential and much of the equivalent arrays would be empty or hold standard default values. There is no space to discuss all the possible kinds of data structure, and indeed no necessity to do so. The guiding principle is to determine how much of the stored information is either null, or predictable in the sense that most items will have a standard or default value. If this is considerable, then it is the programmer's task to find the most suitable data structure to exploit the fact, and the algorithms needed to process the data in that form. Yet again this means recourse to the literature, since there may be standard methods; for example, techniques are well developed to store and handle 'sparse' matrices (that is, matrices most of whose elements are zero) — see for example the paper by Duff cited in the reading list. Another relevant factor to be taken into account is whether a language can be used which lends itself to handling data structures other than simple arrays.

Two further techniques are worth mentioning. One is the possibility of sharing store between two large data sets required disjointly in two different parts of the program, already mentioned in Section 3.3. The other is the use of *packing,* for example where arrays of zeros and ones are compressed into the smallest possible space by putting (say) 16 elements into one 16-bit word, or where each character of a character array is put into a single byte. Some languages include facilities for this (for example **bits** and **bytes** modes in Algol 68, the *pack* and *unpack* procedures in Pascal) whereas others may need library functions or even specially written machine-code modules. Special-purpose packing can often be arranged by the programmer himself. For example, if the range of values in an integer array is small, items can be packed by arithmetic, several to one integer location, to exploit the full range of integer values provided. All this is very language-dependent (Algol 68, for example, provides **short** modes to do some of this kind of thing automatically) and system-dependent.

It may nevertheless be that, whatever one does, the data outruns the available store; indeed, this may be obvious from the outset. In this case it is inevitable that backing store such as magnetic tapes or disk files will have to be used during the processing. (What happens when even this is not enough, or when a small system has no backing store, will be discussed later.) It is still worth considering changes of algorithms and data structures and the use of packing methods, to minimize the disk transfers or tape handling, but if you find yourself in such a position you will have to decide whether the effort required would be justified by the benefits.

One thing which should always be looked at, however, is whether a suitable algorithm exists which conveniently handles only part of the data. The statistics examples given earlier are an extreme case of this, but there may be methods which can deal with sections of the data at a time and which minimize the number of times each section has to be handled — a very important factor, as we shall see. In numerical work, for example, there are methods involving the partitioning of matrices, a technique not so well known as it should be. It may that a large data set has some sort of structure, that is, that it can be divided into subsets (perhaps at several levels) each of which can, for at least some purposes, be conveniently handled together. The processing and the use of backing store should be organized to exploit this structure, if at all possible.

A great deal will depend on the nature of the backing store and the files which can be kept on them. Magnetic tapes can hold a lot of information, but this must be filed and processed sequentially for efficient operation. This is because non-sequential processing, or repeated processing of the same data, involves non-productive forward or backward tape winding at mechanical speeds. The time to switch to data not immediately under the reading heads is therefore long for magnetic tape compared with core or other random-access store, and even compared with cyclic store like magnetic disk. All this implies corresponding constraints upon the data structures and algorithms used.

Magnetic disk and other random-access or cyclic access devices can, in contrast, support both sequential (serial) and random files, thus placing correspondingly fewer constraints upon the programming. Of course, other considerations enter — the size of the files, speed of access needed, cost, etc. Often the programmer himself is not directly responsible for decisions on these matters, but it is as well to be aware of what the system overheads are on your system for tape rewinds and forward winds, tape or disk pack mounts and demounts, track changes on moving head disks, and so on. In fact, you may find that the operating system helps you by performing 'system balancing', for example by adjusting peripheral transfers and processor use to achieve the most economical use of the system; but it is always desirable to know what the operating system does and what is left to the programmer to organize. Pride in professional competence should give sufficient incentive, but if it does not, remember that life is often unfair, and you might find yourself blamed for some inefficiency even though someone else ought to have warned you not to use method A now that decision B has been taken!

If magnetic tapes are to be used, the following will be found to be useful guidelines.

1. Avoid tape rewinds as much as possible, and preferably eliminate them altogether if you can.

2. Similarly, try to reduce the mounting and demounting of tapes to a minimum.

3. However, when updating a tape file, it is preferable to copy onto a new tape, making the amendments in the process.

4. Within the limits of items 2 and 3 above, minimize the number of tape drives used.

In connection with item 3, amending a file onto a copy is always worth considering, whether sequential or random, tape or disk, since the old version is retained as backup if anything should go wrong. This 'father and son' technique is often extended, for important files, to 'grandfather, father, son' and even beyond, plus the use of 'archive' files. In many respects this is simpler and safer using magnetic tapes, or exchangeable disks if these are available, and this is the approach to adopt if disk space is at a premium, even to the extent of copying random files to magnetic tape. Provided that the random file is copied back to disk for processing, no harm is done.

Detailed consideration of the techniques of file organization and handling are beyond the scope of this book. The book by S. J. Waters given in the reading list is recommended to anyone who wants to follow this up. You should, of course, make full use of that book and similar sources in the literature if you are working on a project requiring the extensive use of files. You should in any case find out what file storage systems are available, and which store management and file management techniques you should be using on your particular computer. If store management and file transfers are automatic, as for example in virtual memory systems, it is as well nevertheless to be aware, at least in general terms, of how they operate.

Virtual memory systems were introduced in Section 3.3, and if your computer system has this facility it will take care of many of the worries discussed in this section; but Section 3.3 did give an example of why you do need to know how the facility works. As that example showed, virtual memory systems will work regardless of the structure of your data and your problem, but it will work better with some than with others.

It is worth mentioning here that, if your system does not have virtual memory, it can be worth using disk files (not tapes) to provide your own 'virtual memory' for a program, if the structure of the data or problem does not suggest any more specific use of backing store. An example might be where the program has to do repeated scans of large monolithic arrays. In the simplest case, where you have one very large one-dimensional array, the technique involves keeping a suitable section of the array in main store, keeping track of where in the whole array it begins and ends, and checking every array subscript evaluation. When a subscript turns up which is outside the current range, you call a routine to overwrite the section of the array in the main store with the appropriate section of the whole array from the disk file, remembering to update the record of where it begins and ends. You then resume processing from where you left off.

Though extension to multidimensional arrays, several arrays, and even other kinds of data structure is straightforward in principle, it gets complicated in practice and the inexperienced programmer is well advised to get some help. It is worth asking round your installation anyway, since someone may have done something similar in the past, and have routines which you can adapt.

There remains the question of what to do if there is insufficient store even with every economy and with maximum use of backing store. On today's large systems this unlikely to occur, except where backing store, or the maximum share of it which you can be given, is fixed; however, it can still arise on small minicomputer or microcomputer systems, and of course the very tiny systems which have no backing store at all. In such cases the only hope is to try to arrange the computation so that the offline store of data, in some machine-readable form like paper tape or cards, is treated as a kind of 'tertiary store', of effectively limitless capacity but very slow access. The program will then have to be organized on the basis of making the human operator input the required data, at various stages where, if adequate backing store had been available, a file transfer would have been made. The objective must be to make the operations to be performed as simple and as little error-prone as possible, with as few re-inputs of blocks of data as can be arranged. In many cases, updates of the information in this external 'tertiary store' will be required, and will have to take the form of machine-readable output such as paper tape for re-input later in the run if required. It is essential in such systems that all such blocks of data – card decks, paper tape reels, etc – contain machine-readable identification, which is checked on input to guard against the accidental input of the wrong block by the operator. The program should also be made as little vulnerable as possible to any consequences of offline damage to such blocks, for example a tape being torn or a card deck being dropped. Some redundancy may have to be built in, despite the extra time and handling this might involve.

Where exchangeable backing store is available, obviously this should be used, as each unit (tape or disk) will hold much more information, and the access times are much less. The same general principles (minimizing handling, inclusion of identification etc) will, however, still apply. The tapes or disks not actually loaded are still an offline 'tertiary store'. Indeed, magnetic tape in particular is regarded as a form of high-speed input-output as much as a form of backing store, and some systems will not read and write tapes directly to and from main store, using instead a disk buffer area just as for cards, paper tape, terminals etc. It is always important to be clear in your mind whether your input-output is simply that, or a means of access to a 'tertiary store' in the sense described.

As always, the essential thing when having to cope with a large amount of data is to think through the whole problem from beginning to end, considering all the available possibilities instead of simply taking the first which comes to mind or the one which is most familiar, and seeking advice where necessary. In addition, if system operators are to run your program for you, do not dismiss any operating requirements as being 'their problem and what they are paid for'. While your program is running, they as well as the machine are working for you, and it is your duty as an employer to relieve them of unnecessary worry and effort. If nothing else, this is a form of enlightened self-interest. Operators quickly learn to recognize the characteristics of jobs and their owners. In the long run you will be repaid, in goodwill, for being considerate.

Brian Meek

4.3 LARGE PROGRAMS

A large program generally has a memory requirement which approaches or even exceeds the total available memory of the computer on which it is to be executed. Thus a program which is large in relation to one computer may not be considered large in relation to another computer with more available memory. The two main factors which determine the size of a program are the number of statements in the program and the amount of memory reserved by the program for storing data (for example, in arrays). General methods of reducing store requirements, were discussed in Section 3.3, especially the use of dynamic storage allocation for arrays, etc.; and the problems of coping with large amounts of data were further discussed in the previous section of the present chapter. In this section we shall concentrate on the problems caused if the program text itself is very long; that is, if the store requirement to hold the compiled program instructions together with the minimum practical quantity of stored data is very large for the computer in question. (In this context, 'data' is taken to include the variables, arrays etc. explicitly included in the program, but not the temporary working space needed for such purposes as the evaluation of expressions, which the programmer does not directly use.)

As was seen in Section 3.1, a program which consists of more than a few hundred executable statements is generally extremely difficult to debug and check for correctness because of the number of logical paths through the program and the length of each logical path. For the same reasons, this kind of program is usually not easy to modify or develop once it has been written; and when another person needs to make use of it, he or she is unlikely to find it straightforward to understand, an aspect which will be discussed further in Section 5.3. It is therefore absolutely essential, before starting to write any large program, that the preliminary steps of analysing the problem in detail and planning the overall design of the program (described in Chapter 1) are rigorously followed. In particular, a thorough analysis at this stage will often reveal that there is no need to write a large program at all. Instead, it may be possible to break the problem down into a series of well-defined separate steps, and to design several moderately small programs, one for each step, which can be executed as a sequence. The results produced by each of these programs may be written out onto a backing store device (for example to a file on a disk or a magnetic tape) and then read back into the memory by a program later in the sequence which needs to make use of those results as data for its own particular stage of the problem.

Suppose, for example, that you have been able to analyse the problem into four distinct steps, where step 1 generates some results which are required in both steps 2 and 3, and that steps 2 and 3 both produce results which are needed in step 4. Instead of writing one large program to solve the problem, it will generally be much simpler to write four smaller programs A, B, C, and D, making use of the programming principles described in Section 2.4. In step 1, program A is executed and writes its results onto file 1; in step 2, program B reads its data from file 1 and writes its results onto file 2; in step 3, program C reads its data from file 1 and writes its results onto file 3; and in step 4, program D reads its data from files 2 and 3, and generates the final results for the problem. This is illustrated diagrammatically in Fig. 4.3A. Besides reducing the conceptual and practical difficulties associated with large programs, this approach also has the merit that it conserves one of the most valuable computer resources, the amount of available memory, the advantages and benefits of which were fully discussed in Section 3.3.

In some cases, however, the preliminary analysis of the problem may not suggest that it can be readily split up into a sequence of discrete steps, and it may then be necessary to plan and design a single large program. If this is the case then it is essential that the program is designed to be highly modular. That is to say, each specific task performed by the program should be designated as a separate subprogram. Complex tasks should be further subdivided into several subprograms, each of which performs a particular section of the task. This process of repeated subdivision should be continued until each subprogram is conveniently small and has a single well-defined purpose. In this way, a hierarchy of subprograms is constructed. Each subprogram should then be written so that it follows as closely as possible the programming principles described in Section 2.4. The difficulties inherent in writing, testing, debugging, modifying, and understanding a large program will be greatly reduced if modular program design is adopted right from the start. (See also Section 3.1.)

When a large program is being written there are several programming techniques which can be used to reduce the amount of memory required by the program. Firstly, it is important to ensure that the memory space reserved by the program is effectively used, by means of the techniques discussed in Sections 3.3 and 4.2. This will help to reduce the total demand for store from the program and data combined, and may release sufficient space to ease significantly the problems of reducing the program text itself.

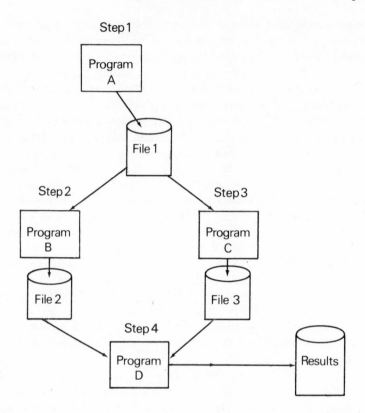

Fig. 4.3A – Achieving the effect of one large program with several smaller ones.

Secondly, it is important to ensure that the program contains no redundant code. Redundant code is essentially of three kinds: 'dead' code, 'idle' code, and 'repeated' code. **Dead code** means a statement or a group of statements which cannot be executed because it does not lie on any of the logical paths through the program. Two common examples of dead code are a subprogram which is never referenced, and a statement or group of statements which can never be executed because it is immediately preceded by an unconditional GOTO instruction and does not carry a label or number by which it can be accessed. All dead code must be eliminated from the program. This is usually not too difficult to achieve, as many compilers can help to detect dead code, and issue warning messages or even delete it automatically – see the discussion on optimizers in Section 3.3.

Idle code, however, is more difficult to deal with. **Idle code** consists of a statement or group of statements which is executed, but which causes no output and has no effect on the subsequent course of the computation. A simple example is an assignment initializing a variable which is subseqently never used (usually a relic of some previous version of the program, which in error was never deleted). The trouble is that such code is very difficult to spot, especially in a long program, though assiduous study of traces and profiles (see Section 3.3) may help to reveal it.

The third kind of redundant code, **repeated code**, occurs when the same text appears more than once in the program, and can be eliminated by rewriting it as a subprogram which can then be called whenever it is needed. However, this should not be used indiscriminately, because a subprogram call does involve system overheads of space and time; unless the length of the repeated code is substantial, or it is repeated many times, the saving of space may be too small to be worth the execution overhead, and may not even exist.

A third method of reducing the amount of memory required by a large program involves using one of the closely-related techniques known as *overlaying* or *segmentation,* provided that one is available on the computer system and language implementation you are using. (It should be mentioned here that these two terms are not standardized, and are consequently sometimes used interchangeably.)

In **overlaying**, the programmer is allowed to divide his program into logical sections called *overlays*. Each overlay is stored separately in compiled form on backing store, except for the so-called *base overlay* (strictly a misnomer as it neither overlays nor is overlaid by any other) which is resident in memory throughout the execution of the program. The base overlay controls the order in which each of the primary overlays is loaded into the memory, executed and then overwritten as the next primary overlay in the sequence is loaded. In many systems, each primary overlay is itself able to load and execute a sequence of secondary overlays, in a similar fashion. Data which needs to be passed between secondary overlays loaded by the same primary overlay may be stored in that primary overlay. Data which needs to be passed between primary overlays, or between secondary overlays loaded by different primary overlays, must be stored in the base overlay. This ensures that only the subprograms and associated data immediately required for execution to proceed are actually resident in the memory at any given time. The effect of the overlaying is therefore to reduce the memory requirement of the program. However, really effective overlaying of complex programs required a great deal of careful analysis and planning.

As a simple example of overlaying, let us consider a program which first reads in a large quantity of data and checks it for validity and consistency, then performs several statistical analyses on the data, and finally prints out the results of the analyses in the form of tables and graphs. This program, if it were considered necessary, could reasonably be written as a base overlay and three primary overlays, A, B, and C. Overlay A would read in the data and check it, overlay B would perform the statistical anaylses, and overlay C would print out the tables and graphs of the results. The base overlay would be used to load and execute each of the three primary overlays in turn, and also to store the screened input data and the results of the analyses. If, however, the statistical analyses contained in overlay B are numerous and complex, then it might well be worthwhile dividing them into several secondary overlays (for example W, X, Y, and Z) each of which is loaded and executed, one at a time, from overlay B. A diagram of this program's residence in the memory would then look something like Fig. 4.3B.

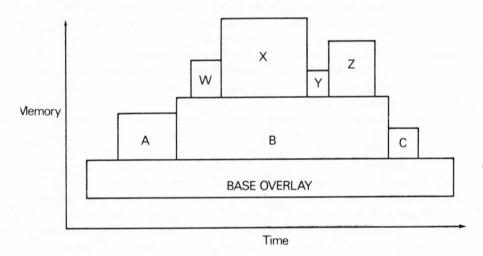

Fig. 4.3B – Memory residence of a simple program using overlays.

The alternative technique, **segmentation**, is very similar both in terms of what the programmer has to do and in its effect. Again the programmer divides his program into logical sections, now called *segments*; the organization of the program segments within the memory is described by a hierarchical tree-like structure, and the main difference between this technique and overlaying is that the loading of a segment is automatic when a part of it is referenced. Fig. 4.3C shows the tree structure for the program in the previous example if it were to be segmented in exactly the same way as it was divided into overlays. R is the root segment which is resident in the memory throughout the execution of the program. When one of the subprograms in segment A is referenced from the root segment, the whole of segment A is loaded from the backing store into the memory above the root segment. When one of the subprograms in segment B is referenced from the root segment, the whole of segment B is loaded into the memory from the backing store, overwriting segment A. Similarly, when a subprogram in segment W is referenced from segment B, segment W is loaded into the memory above segment B. In some systems it is possible to define structures which include several trees springing from different levels in the memory, and this increases the flexibility of the segmentation procedure.

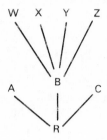

Fig. 4.3C – Tree structure of a simple segmented program.

It can be seen that for this simple example the net effects of overlaying and of segmentation are identical, and indeed the main differences between the two are of implementation, though the form of the implementation also varies quite widely from one computer system to another. The principal advantage of segment-ation is the automatic loading, already mentioned; however, this is offset by the fact that the segment tree structure has to be specified, and loading the next segment tends to be a more time-consuming process than loading the next overlay, though the extent of this depends upon the hardware. In fact, the differences are of no significance to the programmer using the system, because normally only one or other technique, if either, is offered. If overlaying or segmentation is available, then its use can indeed substantially reduce the memory required by a large program; but it must be stressed again that either technique demands a great deal of care and effort to be applied effectively. They should certainly be used only with the greatest discrimination.

Finally, it is important to recall that there is a large class of computers in which a program can apparently occupy more memory than the total available memory of the computer. These computers are said to possess 'virtual memory'. They were described in some detail in Section 3.3 and mentioned again in Section 4.2. Here it is necessary only to point out that they are particularly suitable for executing large programs, because they effectively remove all con-straints on the maximum amount of memory which a program may require. However, if you are fortunate enough to have access to a computer with virtual memory, you should certainly not allow the apparently limitless amount of memory available to lead you into writing programs which are inefficient in their utilization of the memory. All the techniques which have been described should be used to reduce the memory requirements of all large programs, thus conserving the available memory for other people's programs which are being executed at the same time as your program. A responsible attitude towards minimizing the memory requirement of your own large programs will therefore benefit you and the people who use the computer with you.

Richard Overill

4.4 PROGRAMS WITH LONG RUN-TIMES

Deciding what is meant by a program or its data having 'a large memory requirement', in the terms of the discussion in the last two sections, is relatively straightforward. Determining whether a program's run-time is 'long', however, is much more complicated. For practical purposes what is 'long' in given circumstances depends on a large number of factors. One important factor is obviously processor speed – today's fastest machines are about 1000 times faster than those of ten years ago, although those may still be in service; and what is a long program for an old machine may not be so for a new one. A program which is not a long one for a dedicated minicomputer system might be regarded as 'long' if it is transferred to a heavily-loaded batch system, even if the batch processor is much faster and the actual processor time used by the program is correspondingly less.

In many systems, even if the actual processor time used by a program is quite modest, it may still be regarded as a 'long' program if the elapsed clock time between the start and finish of processing is much greater, because a lot of time is spent waiting for peripheral transfers or operator action. In such cases the relevant factor may be what operations managers tend to call 'MTBI', standing for 'mean time between incidents'. Here 'incident' means a partial or complete breakdown of the system caused by a hardware fault or a bug in the system software, and the MTBI is thus a measure of the reliability of the computer system. What is considered 'long' for a computer system with an MTBI which is not very good may not be considered 'long' on another system where the MTBI is better, even if the processor speeds are the same. Clearly, if the elapsed time needed to process a program from start to finish is larger than the MTBI, or even a substantial fraction of it, the chance of premature interruption by an 'incident' cannot be ignored.

In fact, a programmer seldom has to work out for himself what is 'long' for the particular computer system he has to use; all he has to do is to determine whether his program is going to be classed as 'long' for that system. Of course, a beginner has very little idea what resources will be used by any program. This is something which comes with experience, and even an experienced programmer may take a little time to get used to a new computer system if it is very different from any he has used before. If you are doubtful about your ability in this respect, make a habit of looking at the accounting and statistical information commonly provided by operating systems, particularly the amount of processor or 'mill' time used by the run, and the total elapsed time that the job is in the system (for batch processing) or logged-in time (for an interactive system). Soon you will begin to get some feel for these quantities.

While this will not in itself allow you to judge if a program is 'long' for your system, this information is usually easy to obtain. It may be possible to infer it from the different job categories commonly used in batch operating systems for scheduling and assigning priority. Usually a job requiring more than a certain amount of processor time will be placed in a lower priority or 'background' category — find the lowest priority or 'heaviest resource requirement' category into which the jobs with the longest run-times will necessarily fall, and this will give you the lowest time limit for a 'long' job (unless this turns out to be a 'very long' category and jobs with lower requirements are also regarded as 'long'). To give an idea of what to expect, typical values for a large batch system at the end of the 1970s, based on a processor like the IBM 370/168 or CDC 7600 or ICL 2980, are from 2 to 5 minutes of processor time. Usually at such installations an explanatory document is available describing the job categories, and this may explicitly tell you what a 'long' job is. For an interactive system, again there may be a limit on the length of a logged-in session, at least in 'prime time' (periods of peak demand); and even if there is no specific limit on the processor time used, you will soon learn how much you are likely to get through in the (clock) time available. In any case, for human reasons a period of more than an hour interacting with a program before it has completed a run can be regarded as 'long'.

Even if the local definition of 'long' cannot be easily deduced in such a way, the people running the system will be able to tell you; and in any case a program which will take an elapsed time for execution of a substantial proportion of a working day must be regarded as 'long' for any system if it involves operator intervention. Let us therefore suppose that you do have a program which is definitely 'long' for your system, and consider what problems this may cause, and how to cope with them.

The main problems of a long program are that it may get delayed through being low priority, which may or may not be important, and that it has a greater chance of interruption through error, which certainly is important. The interruption may be because of an 'incident', or through some human error such as incorrect input or a mistake by an operator. It is this aspect we shall mainly be concerned with.

Note that, while a long program may also be a large program (in the sense of Section 4.3), this is by no means always the case. A program can be written in a few lines to search for so-called 'perfect' numbers, that is, positive whole numbers which are equal to the sum of their proper divisors, such as $6 = 1 + 2 + 3$, and $28 = 1 + 2 + 4 + 7 + 14$. These two will be found very quickly, but the next one is 496, and the one after that is 8128. The problem is both that the determination of the divisors takes progressively longer, and that the occurrence of perfect numbers becomes progressively sparser. It is an algorithmic example of the 'combinatorial explosion' mentioned in Section 4.1 as a major problem of heuristic programs; heuristic programs are often long programs for this reason.

If, however, your long program is also a large program, it is possible that the technique of splitting the program into smaller programs (see Fig. 4.3A) will also serve to solve this problem, provided that the splitting can be done in such a way that the time as well as the space required can be effectively divided between the smaller programs. It may be the case, however, that the bulk of the execution occurs in a relatively small section of the program (typically in a set of nested loops), and so this will not help.

Assuming that the problem cannot be so easily removed, the next step is to try to reduce the magnitude of the problem by increasing efficiency, using all the means previously discussed — searching for a more efficient algorithm, using profilers and optimizing compilers, eliminating 'idle' code which is non-productive and whose execution wastes time just as the existence of the code wastes space. These techniques have already been discussed in Sections 1.3, 3.3, and 4.3, and need not be repeated here except to stress that they must not be overlooked. It is surprising how many programmers try to get more machine time, or devise elaborate means to cope with their long-running programs, when simple ways to improve the performance are readily available. Sorting algorithms or search strategies inappropriate to the data, ill-chosen convergence criteria for numerical algorithms, and unnecessary looping are all common faults. An example was cited in Section 3.3 of a program whose execution time was reduced from over 30 minutes to about 2½ minutes by such means. Another example: the program, this time produced in an industrial environment, involved five nested loops whose control variables each ran from 0 to N. The controlled code was thus executed $(N+1)^5$ times, but in fact achieved anything productive only when the sum of the control variables was N; in addition, the code involved repeated calculation by means of a function call of factorials, for a limited range of values. By calculating these in advance and storing them in an array, and replacing the nested loops by I1 from 0 to N, I2 from 0 to N − I1, I3 from 0 to N − (I1 + I2), and so on, the execution time was cut by 98%.

However, if the program still falls into the category of long programs after it has been made to execute as efficiently as possible, then the next step is to build into the program a variety of reliability features which will prevent the program from wasting a lot of processor time in the event of problems arising while it is being executed. These features may be divided into three main groups: fail-safe/restart facilities, input data screening, and monitoring of iterative processes.

We begin the discussion of fail-safe and restart facilities with the not uncommon case where a programmer has to submit a long job to a batch system specifying the maximum allocation of processor time he wants, when in fact he is unable to predict very accurately how much time this particular run will need;

that is, he cannot be certain that the time requested is long enough. If a program does exceed the processor time available to it, then the operating system will normally terminate the program's execution immediately. From the programmer's point of view this action is usually disastrous because it means that most, if not all, of the results so far produced by the program have been lost, and the program will have to be re-run from the start with a larger time allocation. To avoid this, which wastes both computer resources and the programmer's time, the program must be equipped, if possible, to detect when it is close to its time limit, and to write onto some medium suitable for re-input, such as a disk file, sufficient information to enable the processing to be continued from the point of interruption, rather than it having to be repeated from the beginning. This information is often called a 'dump'. Store and register dumps were mentioned in Section 3.2 as records often produced by operating systems in the case of a run-time error; this kind of dump is quite different, and we shall call it a 'restart dump' to avoid confusion.

The program will have to be adapted to accept input to restart a previous run as well as to start a new one from initial data; in effect, we have a situation similar to that in Section 4.3, except that the program now puts information on a file for its own future use. The similarity can be seen in Fig. 4.4A, which illustrates the case when a program has to be restarted twice, though the more general situation is shown in Fig. 4.4B.

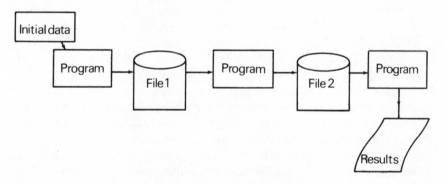

Fig. 4.4A – Program with two restarts.

Although the principles of fail-safe and restart techniques are the same for all programs, there are variations in detail depending on whether the processing is essentially iterative or essentially non-iterative. In the iterative case, the program needs to know at the end of each iteration how much of the allocated processor time still remains. In some systems this information is available as a special function which the program can reference, while in others the time actually used so far is available (in which case the time left can be found by subtracting this from the allocated time, which will have to be provided, for example as an additional item of input data). Once the time remaining is known, this should be compared with the time taken to perform the previous iteration. If there is sufficient left to complete a further iteration *and also to create the restart dump afterwards,* then another iteration should be performed. If not, then the restart dump should be created immediately, a message that the program has been successfully dumped should be printed, and program execution can then be terminated. The time required to create a restart dump clearly depends upon the amount of information which the program will need in order to be able to restart its processing from the next iteration, but experience suggests that this is usually significantly less than the time required to perform a single iteration.

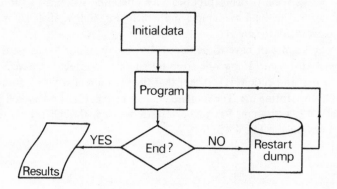

Fig. 4.4B — Program with general restart facility.

Figs. 4.4A and 4.4B indicate that a program set up in this way effectively operates in one of two modes: 'startup' mode when a run is initiated, and 'restart' mode when a run is resumed after a dump. Clearly the design should be sufficiently flexible that a restart dump can be produced in restart mode as well as startup mode, so that the total run can be split up into as many partial runs as necessary. In fact a run can safely be initiated with a time allocation far less than it is known will be needed, which can have two advantages. One is that each partial run may be able to have a higher priority, and so turn round faster; the other is that the programmer may be able, using suitable printouts as well as restart dumps, to monitor progress (for example, a convergence rate) and decide whether to continue it, to abandon it, or even to take some special action (such as invoking a third, terminating, mode at the next restart to complete the total run earlier than would otherwise occur). We shall discuss later how a program may be able to monitor its own progress automatically.

The technique just described can be adapted for other situations. If no special 'clock' function to tell the program about the processor time is available

— or it is wished to avoid its use to make the program more transportable to other systems — a restart dump can be forced after a preset number of iterations. It is then of course necessary to ensure that the initial and any further runs have sufficient time allocation to be sure to reach the next restart dump point; this is usually possible, but is not always easy. In the case of interactive programs, a good method is to include pauses at the ends of iterations, where the user is given the option to continue for one (or more) further iterations, or to generate a restart dump. This gives greater flexibility and the opportunity to exploit human judgement; it can of course be combined with the kind of progress monitoring just discussed.

In the case of a non-iterative process, the implementation of fail-safe and restart facilities is somewhat different from that described above for an iterative process, although the principles are the same. Many long, non-iterative programs are designed to calculate a large number of related quantities successively, using the same algorithm throughout. These programs usually contain one or more extensive loops which are executed once for the calculation of each quantity. To prevent this sort of program from exceeding its time allocation, the amount of time remaining to the job needs to be determined each time one of these loops is executed, and compared with the time required for the previous execution of the loop. If there is enough to execute the loop again and also to create a restart dump afterwards, then one more execution of the loop should be performed; otherwise, a dump should be created immediately. In this case, the dump should consist not only of sufficient information to allow the program to be restarted at the evaluation of the next quantity (for example the current value of the loop count), but also of those quantities which have so far been calculated by the program. However, when the program is subsequently operating in restart mode, it may not be necessary to read in these quantities from the backing store if they are not required explicitly in the remainder of the program. Long programs which do not have an overall loop structure are generally more difficult to equip with fail-safe and restart facilities. Although the principles of time-monitoring and use of backing store remain the same, the actual details of their implementation will depend largely upon the design of the particular program.

Some computer systems offer a facility for automatically dumping and restarting programs at the programmer's request; this is commonly known as a checkpoint dump/restart facility. A checkpoint dump can be requested by the programmer at any point during the execution of a program, and its purpose is to capture the total environment of an executing program by writing to a backing store device all the information required to restart the execution of the program at the next instruction (for example the contents of the memory, registers, file buffers, etc. used by the program). Its effect is simply to take a 'snapshot' of the current state of the executing program. Snapshots were mentioned in Section 3.2 as a debugging aid; here the object is not to provide information to the programmer, but to preserve it for the computer system and make possible a subsequent checkpoint restart. The task of the checkpoint restart is to use the information saved by the checkpoint dump to reconstruct exactly the state of the executing program at the time the dump was taken, and then to set the program in execution again. Thus the combined effect of a successful checkpoint dump and restart is just as though the execution of the program had never been interrupted.

The discussion so far has dealt with the predictable event of a time allocation being exhausted. We shall now turn to the problem of unpredictable interruptions, caused by system 'incidents' or operating errors. These can affect any program, but become especially important if the mean time between incidents (MTBI) is not long compared with the allocated time, or the program is to be allowed to run to completion, however long it takes (because its priority is so high, or the system is dedicated to it), and the expected run-time exceeds the MTBI or is comparable with it.

To overcome this problem, it is first necessary to decide how much processor time you would be prepared to risk wasting if an interruption occurred. We shall call this quantity the critical time. The programming procedure is then to monitor the time used since the program started executing, and when this approaches the critical time, to create a restart dump. Execution of the program is then continued until the processor time used since the previous dump approaches the critical time, when another dump is taken. The process of creating a new restart dump at regular intervals is continued until execution is complete, and if an unpredictable error should occur there is always a sufficiently recent dump from which to restart such that the amount of time wasted is less than the critical time. It can be seen that the method of dealing with unpredictable errors is merely a variation of that used for coping with a time allocation running out. The adaptations for iterative and non-iterative programs, and for batch and interactive systems, and for whether or not the processor time used is available to the program while executing, all carry across.

None of these measures can cope with the situation when a program fails because of errors in input. Data checking (also called validation, or screening) is good practice generally (see Section 2.3) but is especially important with long programs. Nothing is more infuriating than finding that large amounts of computer time, and possibly human time and other resources as well, have been wasted by executing a long program with the wrong data. This applies both when the run 'crashes' through invalid data before completion (for example an input error detected by the system, or a division by zero or other arithmetic overflow), and when the program terminates normally but the results are rubbish. Therefore, as many of the following rules as apply in the particular case should be adopted:

1. Work out in advance as many validation criteria as you can for the input data − whether a given value lies in some numerical range (for example −1 to + 1), whether or not a number must be an integer, how many characters should be in a character string, what characters are expected in some input text, how many data items there are in a given group, etc.

2. Do not forget the possibility that items may be valid individually but not in combination — a trivial example being division by $(a - b)$, where individual checks on a and b may not be sufficient.

3. Read in data as early as other considerations permit, and apply the criteria at once.

4. Allow for automatic system and format checks.

5. If an unreasonable value or impossible item is found, ensure that the program produces an appropriate message and a copy of the offending value (and any others which are related); execution should then terminate, but if possible not before further screening of data is carried out. It is also infuriating to repeat a run wasted by an input error, only to find that another such error occurs shortly afterwards!

6. In an interactive program, invalid data violating an individual criterion (such as range) can usually be corrected at once and the run continued. If there are criteria on combinations of values, try to organize the input so that the whole combination can be re-input if necessary.

7. If data input well into the course of a run cannot be avoided, try to arrange for a restart dump shortly before it occurs, to minimize the time wasted.

8. Consider the possibility of writing a separate data validation program to run before the main program.

9. Always remember that no amount of data validation within the program can eliminate the need for the most stringent possible offline validation, during and after the data preparation stage.

Finally, we turn to the question of performance monitoring. Criteria may exist not only for the validity of data, but for the validity of intermediate and final results, of the kind which, if applied, would have prevented some of the notorious instances of computer errors such as final demands for zero payments, or electricity bills for unnaturally large amounts. Checks on such criteria, valuable in many contexts as are data validation checks, are again especially useful for long programs. We have already noted the value of such 'progress reports' output at the time of restart dumps, but it is worthwhile in other contexts to see if checks on satisfactory progress are applicable, in order to avoid wastage of time, resources, and effort. Violation of such criteria can be followed either by complete termination, accompanied by appropriate output and possibly a full diagnostic dump, or by suspension of execution accompanied again by appropriate output, but this time also by a restart dump, if it is possible that human judgement can be used to decide whether to stop or to carry on.

It is difficult to give general rules for what to do, since what is possible is inevitably very problem-specific; however, the general remarks about the termination of algorithms, given in Section 1.3, are applicable. A very important class of algorithms for which this technique is particularly appropriate, and which often form part of long programs, are those involving non-finite iterations, such as those which occur in many numerical processes. Specially important are those for which achievement of the terminating condition (see Section 1.3) is not guaranteed (for example, a numerical process may diverge or oscillate instead of converging, or may converge very slowly), or may be prone to rounding error (again, see Section 1.3). In such cases, all possible deficiencies in behaviour should be considered and periodic outputs, after every iteration or so many iterations, produced so that they can be detected if they occur. Automatic monitoring should be included in the program unless you are certain that the chances of a particular bad condition occurring are negligible or the overhead of including the check is too great; a test on speed of convergence is almost invariably worth including. Termination because of such automatic monitoring may be very frustrating, and may involve anything from correction of an undetected error in the data, through modification of the initial data or the algorithm, to searching for and adopting a new algorithm; but it will almost always be more satisfactory in the long run than persisting with a long and tedious process which is certainly inefficient and may in the end be totally unproductive.

Richard Overill

4.5 REAL-TIME PROGRAMS

The terms 'real-time', 'online', and 'interactive' have been used, and to some extent still are used, in a variety of different ways, sometimes fairly indiscriminately and sometimes almost interchangeably. It is helpful to begin by getting the concepts clear, at least in the senses with which they will be used here.

Online is a term which is most useful when describing the state of some piece of equipment (such as a peripheral device) physically and logically connected to a computer system. Thus a device may be *online* or *offline*. The term is often extended to activities ('data preparation is done online rather than offline') or to people ('are you online at the moment?') using such devices, especially when such devices are **interactive**. A typical interactive device is the computer terminal, and is capable of communication in both directions between a human user and a computer system to which it is online. Note that a card reader, for example, may be online or offline, but is not interactive; a terminal may be online or offline, but is interactive when it is online. Again, the term 'interactive' can be transferred both to users and to activities using interactive devices. It is also used to describe programs which can be run interactively, and to computer systems which support interactive terminals. Unfortunately such computer systems are sometimes also referred to as 'online systems'.

Part of the trouble arises from over-use of the word 'system'. Any set of interconnected entities (pieces of computer hardware, computer programs, operational rules or methods, people, ideas, etc., possibly in combination) organized into a whole to perform some function or functions can be called a 'system'. Thus we have political systems, transport systems, management systems, and so on; and in computing we have computer systems (consisting of hardware), operating systems (software), and so on. The problem over 'online' is that a procedure for preparing data online through the use of an interactive terminal may be described as a 'online system', and it is not difficult then to transfer this term from the outside, organizational system to the computer system which makes it possible. For the computer system, however, the term 'interactive' is more appropriate. An organizational system which collects data from automatic monitoring devices which are online to a computer is also an online system, but the computer system supporting the devices need not be an interactive system at all, and because of the confusion in terminology it does not help to call it an 'online' system. As we shall see, it is an example of a 'real-time' system.

'Real-time', in the sense in the sense in which we are using it here, is a term applied to particular kinds of programs, though it is possible to transfer it usefully to particular kinds of computer system. A **real-time program** is one which, during its execution, is subject to real-time constraints generated by some external activity or set of activities with which the program (and the computer system executing it) interacts by means of online devices. Examples of real-time constraints are requirements to produce some results by a given deadline, to react to a given input within a specified period, or simply to perform some task as fast as possible. In the well-known case of the steel rolling mill, the control program has to calculate the optimum thickness and cutting size within a certain time so that the rollers and cutters can be set and the task performed before the red-hot steel cools. In missile guidance or traffic control systems, the program must simply react as quickly as possible to the information or instructions it receives.

Most batch or interactive programs are not real-time programs in the meaning intended here. This is not to say that they have no real-time constraints. On a batch system, a payroll program has to run fast enough to allow people to be paid on time; a weather forecasting program has to complete its run well before the time for which it is making a forecast if it is to be of any practical use. However, these constraints, and any operational constraints, are taken into account at the design stage; once the program has been written and is running in batch mode, there is no interaction with external processes. On an interactive system, similar arguments apply. To be sure, there is interaction with the human user of the program, but real-time constraints such as those just mentioned can also in many cases be taken into account at the design stage, or left to the human user to deal with. The same is true of constraints arising from the need to provide an acceptable interface for the human user of the program, for example by ensuring that the user is provided with periodic 'progress reports' when lengthy processing is taking place, instead of leaving him sitting at a terminal with no input or output taking place. Such programs are also not 'real-time' in the sense in which we are using the term.

Note, however, that an *operating system,* of either a batch or an interactive computer system, *is* a real-time program. A batch operating system has to interact with its online peripherals, to know which of its input devices are at any moment ready to input, which of its output devices are ready to receive output, the status of disk or other backing store devices; it also has to interact with its systems operators. (To a computer operator, any operating system is an interactive program, and the program design should be done accordingly, though unfortunately not all designers of operating systems take this 'human relations' aspect sufficiently into account). An operating system therefore has to take decisions, based on the moment-to-moment status of its various devices and its current job queues, in order to maximize its throughput. The decisions are real-time decisions, because the constraints cannot be fully evaluated and allowed for during design. An operating system must also satisfy the secondary real-time constraint of providing a satisfactory response time to the commands of the system operators. An operating system for an interactive computer system has to do this, and additionally provide satisfactory response time to the human users at its terminals, and to its communications lines if the computer concerned is part of a distributed network.

Writing an operating system is a specialized task which falls to relatively few expert programmers. If you are a beginner, it will be some time before you will be able to aspire to such a task, though if you go to work in a computer installation you may be required to understand and help to maintain an existing one. Since the subject is so specialized and complex, it is beyond the scope of this book to consider it in detail; anyone interested should go to the specialist literature, such as James Martin's well-known *Design of real-time computer systems.* (Note that, by this, Martin primarily means what we would call distributed interactive systems).

There is, however, an extremely important class of real-time applications programs, which many more programmers are involved with; the rest of this section will discuss, in very general terms, the special problems that arise with them. They are programs whose purpose is to monitor, and/or control, equipment such as laboratory apparatus or industrial machinery with which it interacts by means of devices like measuring instruments and servo-mechanisms, often interfaced through analogue-to-digital or digital-to-analogue converters (also known as a-d and d-a converters, or simply a.d.c.s. and d.a.c.s) or through microprocessor interfaces. Such programs range from very simple ones to register, store, and (perhaps, but not necessarily) analyse measurements made in a laboratory, to very complex ones to perform traffic control, to fire and guide missiles, or to run an automated factory. The real-time constraints involved are also many and varied, and may apply both to inputs and to outputs.

Consider first the simple case of a pure monitoring system, whose job is simply to record what is happening in the external environment, and perhaps to analyse it to a greater or lesser extent, but not to take any action as a result. Here the real-time constraints will apply only to the inputs. The only output required will be normal computer output to provide information to the human user of what the monitoring system has recorded, and the only constraint on this will be that it should not interfere with the recording process. The principal factors which will determine the real-time constraints in such a case are

— the number of online monitoring devices, and their nature;
— the amount of information which each generates;
— the rate at which the information is generated;
— whether the rate of generation is regular or subject to change, predictable or unpredictable;
— whether the devices, or the activities they are monitoring, themselves determine the times at which the input data will be available, or whether the computer itself has to provide the necessary timing control;
— the minimal amount of post-input processing which will be needed to detect errors, record the information, and so on.

The job of the programmer in a particular instance is to analyse all these factors and to determine which, if any, are likely to cause major difficulties—for example if the data rate is very fast, calling for tight optimization. Commonly an online device will place its input in a buffer accessible to the computer, and set a 'flag' (for example, one bit in a special register on the hardware interface) to show that it has done so. The monitoring program has to take the input and reset the flag bit before the device produces another input. Thus the programmer has to calculate the speed of this operation, and of subsequent processing, and handling of other online devices if any, in relation to the data rate. If the two are comparable, he has an optimization problem, to be solved by tighter coding or, in bad cases, by reducing the amount of post-input processing; or, even, by a change in the hardware.

Even if there is only one online device, there can be problems. For example, the rate at which the input signals arrive may fluctuate in an unpredictable way. On average there may be ample time for analysis, but at the fastest rate there will not be time to complete the post-input processing of one item before the next has arrived. One solution to this is to code the post-processing as a sequence of steps (expressed as interpretable coded instructions or as calls of mini-routines) and then after each input enter a loop which alternately carries out one step and then checks the flag bit to see if it has been set. If this occurs before the processing of one item is complete, the new item is placed on a queue to be processed in its turn. Provided that space is left for a long enough queue and that the data rate does ease up, eventually the processing will catch up with the input. A similar technique can be used if the processing cannot be done item by item, but has to wait until further data is collected.

Certain kinds of hardware do, however, greatly simplify the programming problems, if they are available. On some systems, the online device can access and write into memory directly, without the processor having to be involved and hence diverted from some other task. The availability of an interrupt facility also, as we shall see, simplifies program design; it can, for example, eliminate the need for an explicitly programmed loop to perform post-processing and check for new input of the kind just described.

A *real-time clock* is a valuable, and for some applications essential, device for a computer system performing real-time work. The programmer can make his program interrogate the clock in order to keep track of the passing of time in the external environment; its use may also eliminate the need to perform elaborate calculations of the execution time of critical parts of the program, since this can be timed directly during testing. Obvious uses of a real-time clock include recording the time of arrival of an input signal – which is usually of interest in real-time applications and for some is essential – and for 'sampling' – where items of input data are continually arriving but the monitoring program only takes them at, say, five-second intervals. In the first case, always allow for the delays between the arrival of the signal, its detection, and its timing from the clock. In the second case, ensure for similar reasons that the clock is interrogated frequently enough that your sampling is done at a time within the tolerances allowed by the requirements of the application. Commonly, however, the real-time clock can be set to interrupt at predetermined times or intervals. This eliminates this problem and, indeed, the need for interrogation at all, except for time-recording purposes.

Such a simple monitoring program will clearly have a structure which includes one module to handle the interrogation of the online device, and one (perhaps divided into submodules) to handle the post-processing. How these will be combined into the complete program will depend on the nature of the computer system being used, in particular on whether it possesses an interrupt facility. Since the programming problems are more severe when it does not, this is the case we shall consider first. What will then be needed, to organize the work of the interrogating and the processing modules, is a higher-level control module, which will perform the necessary timing tasks, ensure that the online device is interrogated as necessary, and organize the work of the post-processing module around this. It may also control other activities such as the output of progress reports and summaries.

Where there are several online devices, this structure has to be extended. Each will have its own interrogation module; but, since the post-processing might involve inputs from more than one device, the structure of these modules may be more complex than the two extremes of one for each device, or a single one for all the devices. The control module will inevitably be more complex, since it has to coordinate the handling of several devices, and it may itself have to be split into submodules.

Organizing the timing of the interrogation of the online devices can form a very tricky design problem. One technique which is often useful is that of 'polling', where the control module calls the interrogation modules one by one in a regular cycle. Where the data rates of the devices are comparable, and it is feasible to perform a complete cycle at a faster speed than the input rate of any

device, this usually works very well. It is commonly used in operating systems
handling interactive terminals, for example, though most users of such systems
will have experienced the pauses in taking input which can occur when such a
system is heavily loaded. What this indicates is that the operating system has too
much to handle to be able to keep up the speed of its polling cycle sufficiently
to match the input rate of all the terminals logged in.

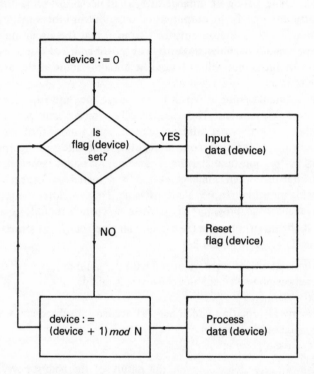

Fig. 4.5A – A simple polling cycle for input devices (see main text). The operator
mod ensures that addition is done 'modulo N'; that is that (N−1)+1 will give 0
and so restart the cycle.

Clearly, polling is an especially useful technique when the data rates of
devices are unpredictable, though if the rates vary greatly between devices more
complex polling cycles may be needed so that the faster devices are polled
more frequently. Polling may also be the simplest way of handling devices even
if they are predictable in data rate; rather than working out a complicated
structure of interrogation allowing for different speeds, you pay the overhead of
unnecessary polling of the slow devices, in order to gain simplicity of control
structure. If, however, data is to be sampled rather than collected, the timing
controlled by a real-time clock, and the sampling has to take place at different

speeds for different devices, then there may be no alternative to working out a pattern of calls to match the requirements. Even here it may be possible to perform a regular sampling cycle and 'throw away' unnecessary samples, if the overhead can be afforded.

So far we have considered simply a recording and analysis system, but some monitoring systems also act as warning systems, to alert human operators if something is going wrong or a dangerous situation has arisen. In some cases it may be sufficient merely to output a message, but in others this may involve real-time constraints on the output; for example, that the alarm must be raised within a few seconds to minimize damage or, possibly, avoid a disaster. Ensuring that this constraint is met will of course be a major factor in the design of the monitoring program.

This is a suitable point at which to introduce the 'interrupt' facility which has been mentioned earlier. This is essentially a means whereby some device like an online monitor or a real-time clock can cause a transfer of control within the processor to a different control register, thus interrupting the previous sequence of instructions and starting a new one. An online device may be set to trigger an interrupt when some condition is detected — for example, some quantity being measured reaches a critical value. This simplifies the programming because it enables the programmer to write a separate module to handle the interrupt. If the interrupt occurs because of an emergency, the structure of such a module, at its simplest, would be:

1. Save the contents of registers shared with the main program (so that normal processing can be resumed once the alarm is raised).
2. Raise the alarm.
3. Record any information which may be needed for subsequent investigation of the cause of the emergency.
4. Revert to main program.

The details will vary depending on the nature of the emergency and of the alarm. In some cases (4) may have to await a human command; some emergencies are so dire that (1) and (4) are redundant!

This also shows how interrupts can help in ordinary monitoring, as well as in emergency cases. If an ordinary input generates an interrupt, or the real-time clock is set to generate an interrupt, as mentioned earlier, the interrogation modules and the processing modules can be written almost independently, and certainly without the need for an overall control module to determine the timings etc. (though an overall module may be needed for other purposes, for example to assess whether a laboratory experiment is going according to plan, or to produce reports and summaries).

Clearly, a problem could arise if several different activities were able to generate interrupts in an uncontrolled way — in particular if an emergency interrupt were to be prevented from raising an alarm because it was itself suspended as a result of a normal, monitoring interrupt from another device. For this reason, interrupt facilities normally include a method of priority ordering, so that 'emergency' interrupts can get top priority and routine interrupts lower priority. This means that routine interrupts can break into background post-processing when everything is going normally, but have to wait for completion of higher priority tasks if earlier interrupts are being processed; also, higher priority interrupts can break into the processing of lower priority ones, which are resumed only when processing of the higher priority one is complete. Computer systems with this kind of facility might well provide several different levels of priority, and it will be one of the tasks of the programmer to decide at what priority level to set his various modules.

It will be apparent from this, and from some earlier points, that the programmer of a real-time system may well need to know rather more about the hardware of his computer, and of the various online devices, than a beginner on a programming course is required to do, and than a programmer working in other environments is likely to have to do. This is one factor which tends to make programming for real-time applications rather more demanding than working in the average 'programming job shop'.

Where a real-time program has to provide responses to, or exercise control over, the external environment with which it interacts, many parts of the earlier discussion carry over. There will be online output devices, logically if not physically distinct from the input devices, and modules will be needed in the program to communicate with them. Processing modules will be needed to determine what outputs are to be produced, and the control module will have to organize the timing of these outputs. The real-time constraints on the outputs, as for those on the inputs, will take various forms. An output may be required as fast as possible, or within a given time, or at a specific time, or at an optimum time which the program has to determine. The first two kinds of requirement are met by code optimization, and the third can be met with the aid of a real-time clock; these are fairly obvious kinds of requirement, but the fourth may be more obscure at first sight. A simple analogy is provided by a child's swing. Its motion can be controlled by pushing, but a push may reduce or maintain or increase its oscillation, depending on when it is applied. Some control applications involve keeping things steady, and if a deviation occurs from some target value, an adjustment has to be made. Simple instances (which do not need a computer) are the use of a gyroscope to maintain a direction, or of a thermostat to maintain a temperature. That control exercised at the wrong time can maintain or build up oscillations is a property, variously known as 'resonance' or as 'positive feedback', which is possessed by many physical systems. Hence it is often important to know, when designing control systems of any kind, whether the phenomenon is likely to occur. If it is, then timing calculations to govern the control outputs may well be needed in the program and, possibly, additional monitoring or processing to try to determine what effect on the external system the control outputs have had, and in particular whether there is a resonance effect.

This, it must be stressed, is just one example of a need for timing calculations, and just one example of the kind of problems which may arise when writing control programs. It should have made it apparent that the difficulties of writing such programs are, in general, of a different order from those of writing a purely monitoring program: a control program with one online input and one online output is quite likely to be harder to design than a monitoring program with two online inputs. Space, and the complexity and wide variety of the subject, precludes anything more than this very general – indeed, almost superficial – discussion, but at least it should have given you some idea of what to expect if you are called upon to write real-time programs.

Everything so far has been concerned with the problems that arise at the stages of analysis and design. In concluding this section it is worth saying a little more about the later stages of program writing and development. First, various languages exist which are designed for real-time applications, or at least to aid the writing of real-time programs. Because real-time applications often involve handling of information at the bit level, such languages generally provide facilities for manipulating machine words, parts of words, and individual bits. Furthermore, since real-time constraints are sometimes very severe indeed, languages often provide simple means to drop down into machine code if hand optimization at that level is needed to satisfy these constraints. For example, hand optimization may be able to take advantage of within-register operations in situations where the high-level language compiler might, for reasons of generality, use less efficient operations using store transfers, etc.

It is for such reasons that Coral 66, the oldest real-time language in wide use, has no explicit real-time features at all, but simply provides the framework for writing real-time programs. It is based on Algol 60, but the least efficient features (in machine terms) of that language are removed, and means added for bit-level data handling, and for dropping down to machine level virtually anywhere. Everything else is left to the implementation and to the programmer. Later languages, such as RTL-2 (which has numerous features akin to features of Algol 68) and the forthcoming American Department of Defense language Ada (a derivative of Pascal) do contain explicit real-time features. Real-time versions of other languages such as Fortran and Basic are also in existence. Space precludes discussion of the languages in detail, and would probably not be helpful since in many cases no more than one will be available. In fact, despite the development of such high-level languages, many real-time programs do still have to be written wholly, rather than just partly, in assembly language. This is much less common than it was in the case of minicomputers or larger systems, but can still occur with microcomputers, which are increasingly used for this kind of work because of their low cost.

Finally, let us consider the testing of real-time programs. The general techniques of testing and the idea of validating programs rather than debugging them were discussed in Chapter 3. However, real-time programs pose some special problems. Because of the semi-independent nature of the interrupt and processing modules, it is difficult to predict the way in which they will combine and be executed in time sequence. This can lead to obscure timing errors which only appear under certain conditions, were not discovered in testing, and cannot be reproduced. For this reason alone, thorough validation of a real-time program is vital.

For a program of this kind, a modular structure is, very clearly, especially helpful. The handling modules for the various online devices can be tested separately, to ensure that communication between program and device is satisfactory. The processing modules can be tested with simulated data, and the control module similarly tested under a simulation of the operating conditions. Testing the program in its entirety may require a full-scale simulation, with simulation modules generating the inputs and computing the responses of the actual external environment to the outputs produced by the control program. There may even be a case for having such modules written by a completely different team of programmers, so that the simulation should not inadvertently make assumptions about the nature of the real-time program being tested. The reason why this is so important is that it may not be practicable to try out the real-time program in an actual environment in advance − programs written for the space exploration projects are an obvious example − or to test emergency modules in actual emergencies. It might be hard, say, to justify deliberately overheating a nuclear reactor simply to check that the monitoring and control program works properly in such an emergency! In cases like that, of course, it is vital that as many fail-safe procedures be built into the program as possible, since the consequences of a failure could be disastrous. Similar considerations might apply for reasons of cost rather than of danger; for example, many industrial real-time programs using microprocessors are now reproduced in their thousands on ROM (read-only memory) chips; it is extremely important that such programs are, as nearly as the programmers can make them, absolutely right before the ROMs are produced.

A great deal of advice has already been given in this book about what to do when starting on a project. In addition, however, when you are asked to write a real-time program for the first time, you will find it worth while to do the following:

1. Read, thoroughly, the most up-to-date literature you can find on the detailed techniques of real-time programming.
2. Learn, equally thoroughly, the features of the external system which your real-time program will be monitoring or controlling, with particular attention to the kind of data which will be generated, and its rate, and (in the case of a control program) the way it behaves under the kind of control signals your program will be producing.

3.   Discover the essential features of the computer system you will be using, especially the timing characteristics of the hardware, how the online devices work, how they communicate with the processor, and what interrupt facilities there are.

4.   Investigate what real-time languages are available, and if there are any other software tools which may be useful, such as aids to setting up simulations, or cross-assemblers or cross-compilers which enable programs to be developed on larger computers with better diagnostic and support facilities, and then transferred to the real-time machines which will actually run them.

Above all, do not always take on trust everything which the manuals tell you; and, do not be afraid of asking advice from someone experienced in real-time systems. However good you may be at conventional programming, you will not necessarily foresee all the snags!

Brian Meek

CHAPTER 5

Other People

Until now, we have been concerned in this book with helping you to adopt good practice when writing your own programs. We have discussed how to approach a problem, how to plan and code a program and get it to work, how to make it efficient, and how to overcome special kinds of difficulties. All this advice has been directed at you as an individual programmer working on an individual project. However, reference has been made from time to time to the desirability of obtaining advice and assistance at various stages from other people. These remarks have mostly been relevant to all kinds of programming activity, even when the problem is of your own devising and the program is being written for you and you alone to use. In this chapter we want both to bring all these various interactions with other people together, and to extend the discussion to the cases − much more common − where the programmer has definite relationships with and obligations to other people in the course of his work, such as when he is writing programs which people other than himself will use, or is working on a project not on his own, but as one of a team. The second section of this chapter draws together and elaborates the various points made earlier about seeking advice. The third deals with the problems which you may have to face if asked to take over a program which someone else has written, while the fourth is concerned with working as one of a team, instead of simply on your own with only yourself − or only yourself and the requirements of a supervisor or a client − to think about.

Before all this, however, we deal first with the topic which is much the most important as far as other people are concerned, the essential prerequisite if other people are to be able to work with you, to understand what you are doing, and to use the programs which you produce: the question of documenting your program.

5.1 PROGRAM DOCUMENTATION

Documentation is probably one of the most maligned aspects of computer programming. Most programmers, having written, tested, and implemented a program, are only too ready to move on to their next project with a sense of relief. On the other hand, users of programs complain all too frequently that the documentation is incomplete, inaccurate, or inappropriate. It is rare that the only user of a program will be its author; and without details of how to run it, what the method of solution is, what the input/output requirements are, it is worse than no program at all. To paraphrase Leeds and Weinberg's remarks in *Computer Programming Fundamentals* — 'there are many ways of misunderstanding what a program should do and only one way of understanding correctly'. Good documentation is the user's primary aid to understanding. Without it, his chances of misunderstanding the program and hence of using it incorrectly are greatly increased.

Given that the purpose of documentation is to guide the user to a full understanding of the program and how to use it correctly, at what stage should the documentation be produced? In all too many cases, it is produced as an afterthought at the end of the project. Consequently, it usually consists of a hastily annotated listing, plus a minimum of guidance on running the program. Although this type of information is necessary, it is not sufficient, especially where the potential user of the program is not its author. For instance, what does the program do? From such documentation, it would be very difficult to establish what the program does do, particularly if the source is full of obscure code and it has been written in an unstructured manner.

We thus come back to the question 'at what stage should the documentation be produced?'. There is only one fully satisfactory answer. Since a program which cannot be used correctly is worthless, the documentation is an integral part of the program: hence its production should start when production of the program starts, as was said right at the beginning in Section 1.1, and should not be finished until the project is completed. Seen in this way, the documentation will be in a changing state until the final version of the program has been produced. It will serve a useful purpose for the programmer while he is working on the project, allowing him to keep a record of his aims and objectives, to note his changes and the reason for them, and to provide a constant source of reference for the end user (where he is other than the programmer) to ensure that what the user requires and what the programmer is producing are one and the same thing. The very fact that the programmer is documenting his work as he progresses will help to prevent any occurrence of the kind of situation illustrated in the 'swing' cartoon (see frontispiece). We hope you never get into such a situation, but if you do, at least make sure that it is not your documentation (or lack of it) that is responsible!

We saw at the beginning (Sections 1.1 and 1.2) that discussing the problem with others, and reading round the subject, are an important preliminary to writing the program. The first piece of documentation associated with the program, as we saw then, should be the 'project specification' — perhaps not the very first version produced, but the version finally agreed upon between all concerned

– perhaps, as we saw, the programmer's own statement of what he sees the project to be, which others concerned have accepted. We saw in Section 3.1 how important a correct specification is in the prevention of errors – it ensures that the program is solving the right problem.

This project specification, though possibly subject to changes of detail and presentation, will remain throughout the project and become part of the final documentation, since it incorporates one of the most fundamental features – the statement of what the program does. Whoever is to use the program, it is essential that this piece of documentation exists.

However, what further documentation is needed clearly depends a great deal on who is to use the program in future. If the author can be certain that he will be the sole user of the program, his requirements will be minimal. The documentation, in his case, should remind him of what the program does and how it does it, and should provide him with the means of verifying that it is working correctly. This is necessary because computer systems are subject to change. There is no reason to assume that because a program worked on one day in one environment, the same program will produce the same results in what seems to be the same environment on another.

However, where the program will be used by people other than its author, more documentation than this will be required. Because the complexity of programs and their use varies so widely, it is impossible to define exactly what should be produced in each case, but it is possible to state some broad principles which should be adhered to. The first of these is to apply rigorously whatever standards prevail in your local installation for things like format, notation, terminology, content, etc. This will make your documentation easier to use for those familiar with the local conventions.

As has already been stated, the purpose of documentation is to make the program easier to understand and to use. This applies to all aspects of the use of the program, whether by a user who wants results from it, an operator who has to run it for him, or a programmer who has to maintain or modify it. In the light of these various categories of use, different levels of documentation can be distinguished:

– the functional specification:
    what the program does for the user.

– the program specification:
    how to use or alter the program.

– operating procedures:
    how to run the program.

– test and maintenance procedures:
    how to test the program.

Programs vary so much that it is only possible here to provide a check-list of items which might reasonably be included at each level:

Functional specification
> What the program does:
>> the problem it solves;
>> the method of solution;
>> input data expected;
>> output produced;
>> references to the literature.

Program specification
> Functional specification (see note 1 below).
> Detailed description of method of solution.
> Flow-chart (see note 2 below).
> Listing.
> Language and compiler details.
> Libraries or external modules used and description of parameters.
> Requirements for numerical accuracy.
> Details of file handling.
> Interactive and/or batch use (see note 3 below).

Operating procedures
> Hardware requirements:
>> type of computer;
>> minimum and/or maximum core size;
>> peripherals;
>> backing store.
> Data preparation requirements.
> Instructions for actually running the program.

Test and maintenance procedures
> Program specification (see note 1 below).
> Test data.
> Results using test data.
> Cross reference list of variables used in program.
> Hierarchy of modules used in program.
> Loader map.

Not all of these items will be relevant for all programs. On the other hand, for some programs they may not be sufficient; for example, the operating procedures for a real-time control program may need to include safety instructions. It will be seen that the boundaries between the levels are not rigid, and in particular cases it may be possible to merge them — for a small program a single document may be sufficient. The following additional points can be noted:

1. It will be seen that a particular overlap is the inclusion of 'functional specifi-cation' in the list for the program specification, and 'program specification' in turn in the list for test and maintenance procedures. In some cases this may not be necessary. In others it will, and it might make sense to merge, say, the functional and program specifications, or to produce two documents

one of which is contained wholly in the other, or a functional specification and a program specification document which must be read in conjunction with it. In yet others, it may be sufficient to include a summary of, or relevant parts of, the functional specification in the program specification.

2. Flow charts were invented as an aid to program design many years ago, before the development of high-level languages and the establishment of the principles of structured programming. Many now find them superfluous, especially when a language is used which aids structured programming; meaningful identifiers, liberal use of comment, and the control structures of the language are sufficient to make the program understandable. Indeed, some go so far as to claim that conventional flow charts (though not the more modern 'structure charts') actually encourage unstructured programming. However, some do still find the visual representation of flow an aid to understanding, which is why some diagrams have been included in this book (see Section 1.3 in particular), and why documentation standards often require their inclusion. Even if you do not yourself find flow charts a help, be prepared to include them in your documentation as a help to others. (See also Section 5.3.)

3. If a program is wholly interactive, its documentation will be considerably different from that of the equivalent batch program, mainly because a good interactive program will help to guide the user through its facilities while he is using it. However, the total information available, within the program and in the accompanying documentation, is much the same, and the documentation should contain at least a summary of the facilities and how to use them.

4. Remember to update the documentation whenever the program is modified. (See Section 5.3.)

For almost all users of computers, the machine is no more than a means to an end, not an end in itself. Packages and libraries are being increasingly used, in preference to 'one-off' programs, for the solution of many problems. Especially when producing that kind of software (though it is a good general rule) the programmer must make it as easy to use as possible. Producing high-quality documentation is a significant part of this process. You will yourself many times use software written by others; write your documentation as you would wish to find it in such cases — 'do as you would be done by'.

Patricia Heath

5.2 SEEKING ADVICE

In this section, we consider working with other people in the context of seeking advice. All programmers, from the novice to the most experienced, need help from time to time — as has been seen earlier in the book. It should be noted that in programming, 'advice' means 'help' — help in solving problems.

The two principal sources of advice are people and printed material. This section will concentrate on people, as printed material has been discussed in Section 1.2. For the programmer working more or less on his own, advice may be sought from advisors, consultants, or friends. Where the programmer is working as part of a team, advice will generally be given by another member of the team. This situation will not be considered further here.

If the programmer is working at a University or Polytechnic, or through a computer bureau, he will usually find that there is a formal advisory service attached to the installation. In this case, not only are the advisors readily identifiable, they are also employed to help programmers with their problems. Advisors have experience of helping programmers, and if they cannot solve your problem, or help you to solve it, they should be able to indicate other people to see, such as consultants, or further sources of information.

Consultants are either professional computer people who do not normally act as advisors, or academic staff with specialized knowledge of computing techniques. Advice would usually be obtained from consultants only after being referred from the formal advisory service. Although consultants may well be able to provide the best possible advice, they will certainly have their own work to do: if you do need advice from them, be prepared to make, and keep, an appointment to see them.

The advice to be got from friends obviously depends on the friends! However, discussing your problems with computing colleagues or with fellow students following the same course may well prove helpful both to you and the friends.

Before considering the various stages at which advice may be needed in developing a program, it should be emphasized that the more you think about a problem before seeking advice, the more easily will you understand the solution, and this will help your computer programming. If you have to seek help from a consultant, you must certainly make a good attempt to sort out the problem first. Of course, as you gain experience as a programmer, you will find that the kind of advice you require changes. Equally, you will learn where to get the advice most suited to a particular problem.

As has been shown in earlier sections, advice is needed before any programming is done, and is first required when a programming project is being set up. Although printed sources can provide help on suitable techniques, available software, and machine capabilities, this help may not be sufficient. An advisor will give you more specific information about what is available and the constraints you may encounter, and he may also be prepared to give a certain amount of help in the design of your program. If you need to use very sophisticated techniques, the advice of a consultant could well prove to be invaluable at this stage. The help to be obtained from friends at the start of a project is mainly confined to helping you to clarify your ideas; it is unrealistic to expect much constructive help from other novices.

A number of problems may arise once a program has been written and is running, or nearly so. These fall into three broad categories.

The first is the straightforward programming error: the program cannot be compiled because of a syntax error in one or more of the statements. Theoretically, this kind of problem should be solved by reference to the computer manufacturer's manual for the language, or some similar guide. Most compilers print out some message when a syntax error is found, and although these can vary from the explicit 'statement number 23 never referenced' to the notorious 'syntax error before line 0', they will generally attempt to indicate the kind of error and where it has occurred. However, a programming novice may well need help from an advisor. In this case, if a complete listing of the program, with error messages (and the deck of cards on which the program is punched, where relevant), is taken to the advisor, a solution should readily be found. If an advisor is not available and you are unable to solve the problem with the help of the manual, you should discuss the problem with your colleagues. If the program has been written in a new, complicated language, then it may be necessary to go to a consultant, although in general such people may not be sympathetic when approached with syntax errors, as they will expect you to have a thorough grasp of the language you are using, and be capable of sorting out that kind of problem without their help.

The second kind of error occurs once the program has been compiled and is being executed: for some reason, it fails to complete its run. When seeking advice in this case, the following points may be made. First, try to identify the error. Programs may fail because the data has been forgotten or because not enough time was requested for the program to complete its run. Of course, even if the error can be identified, the solution may not be obvious; but here, as with syntax errors, an advisor, or printed sources such as system manuals, should be able to provide the answers. If you cannot identify the error, gather together as much information about the program and the error as you can before approaching an advisor or, if necessary, a consultant. The information should include as much of the following as possible:

1. a listing of the program that went wrong, with a note of what has been changed since the last successful run, if any;
2. a cross-reference map of the program: this is usually produced by the compiler and gives a list of the variables, statement labels, and so forth used by the program and the locations at which these were stored in the computer;
3. a loader map: this is produced when the compiled program is loaded, that is, put into the computer immediately before execution. It will give a list of all routines used;
4. the output that was produced by the program on its run, including the system dump or printout, if any.

If an advisor cannot identify and correct the error with the help of this information, he will at least suggest ways of investigating the error further, or will refer you to a consultant.

The third kind of error occurs when the program does not produce the answers that are required. If it produces only partial results, or if it just stops without producing any results at all, it is best to treat it as an error of the second kind and go to an advisor. If, however, the answers are actually wrong, then the error may well be complicated. Before seeking advice in this case, review the program development and debugging. If that was satisfactory, you may need to review the actual technique that is being used. Even if the problem has not been previously discussed with a consultant, if it remains insoluble, and the technique is under suspicion, a consultant's advice should be sought. Alternatively, 'talking the program through' with a colleague may give a clue to what has gone wrong. 'Talking through' a program, which means working through it line by line as though you were the computer, is frequently the best way of locating an otherwise intractable error; it is really too time-consuming to be done by an advisor or a consultant, but can be done either with a colleague or on your own. (See Section 3.2.)

In this section, we have so far considered seeking advice in the context of program writing. There are two other situations in which advice may have to be sought. The first is the use of a package or library. This is mainly covered by the section on using the literature (Section 1.2), though Section 5.3, on other people's programs, which follows, may also be relevant. The second, where Section 5.3 should certainly be consulted, is if you are contemplating transferring information, either programs or data, from one installation to another. In this case it is strongly advised, in your own interest, that you seek advice at both the issuing and the receiving installations before taking any action.

Finally, three important points: first, do not be ashamed of seeking advice: there is nothing wrong in getting errors in a program and needing help to sort them out. Second, make every effort to understand *why* the advice you have been given solves the problem; unless you do, your programming will not improve, even if your program does. Third, having gone to all the trouble of getting and understanding the advice, *do follow it*. This last point is the most important of the three.

Carol Hewlett

5.3 OTHER PEOPLE'S PROGRAMS

Understanding

It is very probable that, at some time in its life, a given program will be used, maintained, or modified by someone other than the programmer(s) who originally wrote it, either by design, in the case of libraries and packages, or because the original author may have left the organization, or have moved to another project or department whence he is unable to return to his creation. Clearly, if the program is at all important, it should not be abandoned, and so another programmer must set to work on it. Software may be purchased or commissioned from outside the organization, but maintained internally. In academic environments, where the ownership of programs is not closely related to profit considerations, the high cost of writing new programs encourages plagiarism. Provided that this is carried out openly, legally, and honourably, it affords a means of providing necessary software at minimal cost.

Whatever the reason for a program being used by other people, the more easily the program can be read and understood, and the better documented it is, the more easily the program can be used. Two important factors affecting readability are the size and complexity of the program. As has been discussed (see Section 2.4) structured programming techniques reduce the size and complexity of programs to manageable proportions; hence the more structured the program, the more easily readable it will be.

The readability of a program also depends on the style and techniques used by the original programmer or programmers. As in English prose, the style of writing can illuminate or obscure the ideas which are expressed. Idiosyncratic techniques that are quite understandable to the original author may be more efficient, and, being familiar, may be less prone to error; but they can mar the readability of a program. Comments should not indicate what the various statements do, but rather why they do it.

One of the techniques discussed earlier in the section on program debugging (Section 3.1), that of the 'programmer peer review', can help with readability when the program is written, because the author is then forced to explain obscure code passages to his colleagues. Since this method increases the number of people who know and understand the program, it may even obviate the need for a new programmer to learn about it.

The moral for program designers and authors should be clear: programs should be written so that they may be easily understood. If they are not, then the resulting difficulties can subsequently be overcome only by intensive and sometimes inspired work.

Post hoc documentation
One of the most important aids to understanding other people's programs is good documentation (see Section 5.1). Alas, all too frequently such documentation for a program is not available, and the process of understanding then rests partly on the production of post-hoc documentation — documentation written after the event. This is a more difficult task than documenting the program as it is written. Perhaps the only merit of such documentation is that, properly written, it will describe what the new user needed to know to understand the program, rather than what the original author thought the new user would need to know.

The first step, in producing post-hoc documentation, is to obtain a listing of the program, preferably one that is well laid out and has plenty of space for annotation. If a suitable listing is not available, some compilers will produce output in which source code is tided up by indentation and intelligent pagination. Alternatively, there are special purpose layout programs which may be used. An example of this is shown in Fig. 5.3A. Indentation is particularly useful in highlighting conditional and iterative clauses. If these clauses are long, then without indentation it may be difficult to see where they end. To separate individual modules, each one should start on a new page of the listing. This then is the basic text of the program. If there is a description of the program or module, the program text can now be matched against the narrative. If no description exists, then the task of understanding will be harder and additional aids may have to be used.

Whatever their merits for use with well structured code, flow charts provide a useful visual representation where the program structure is complex. If one can be produced, it is another useful aid to understanding another person's program. While the flow chart may be constructed automatically — there are a number of flow-charting programs in existence — a hand drawn chart may be more useful. Like the comments in a well written program, the flow chart should show, not only what the program does, but also why. This is not always possible for a flow-charting program which can only use the comments and statements in the source code. But, because of the time needed for producing flow charts by hand, it may not be practicable or necessary to chart the entire program. The optimal solution may be to produce an automatic flow chart for the whole program, and then improve it for individual complex passages by hand.

A well laid out, annotated listing, with a more or less detailed flow chart, will help to show the logical flow of the program, but the variables named and their use may still be obscure. The production of a comprehensive table of the variables used in each module, as described in Section 5.1, would be another useful aid. Such a table should indicate whether a value is assigned to the variable as a result of an input operation or an assignment statement, or whether its existing value is used in some expression or an output operation. Clearly there are some occasions where the usage cannot be determined solely from an inspection of a single program module. Global variables which can exist and be altered outside the module (for example COMMON variables in Fortran) are a potential source of confusion. Similarly, it is reasonable to assume that variables which are used to transfer information between modules will be used and may be changed within those modules.

Other techniques, usually associated with program debugging, may also be employed to help unravel particular intricacies. These include snapshots and various levels of program tracing, and are discussed in detail in Section 3.2. However, because of the effort involved in interpreting the results, they fall into the category of desperate measures and should only be used as a last resort when all else has failed.

So, many of the aids to understanding are directed towards the production

```
C                                                                   6270
C...   CHECK FOR PRESENCE OF ALL FEATURES                           6280
    60      DO 130 MFEAT = 1, NFEAT                                  6290
            MHITT(MFEAT) = 0                                         6300
            J = MCHARS(MFEAT)                                        6310
            JPT = 71                                                 6320
C...   BUMP POINTER AND TRY NEXT FEATURE WHEN END OF REFERENCE       6330
    70      JPT = JPT + 1                                            6340
            IF ((JPT + J) .GT. IPT) GO TO 130                        6350
C...   TRY TO MATCH NEXT FEATURE STRING                              6360
            DO 80 I = 1, J                                           6370
            II = JPT + I                                             6380
            IF (MREF(II) .NE. MFETUR(MFEAT,I)) GO TO 70              6390
    80      CONTINUE                                                 6400
C...   FEATURE STRING FOUND. NOW CHECK DELIMITERS                    6410
C...   PRECEDING DELIMITER                                           6420
            K = MDEL1(MFEAT,1)                                       6430
            IF (JPT .EQ. 72 .OR. K .EQ. 0) GO TO 100                 6440
C...   CHECK THROUGH DELIMITER SET                                   6450
            K = K + 1                                                6460
            II = MREF(JPT)                                           6470
            DO 90 I = 2, K                                           6480
            IF (II .EQ. MDEL1(MFEAT,I)) GO TO 100                    6490
    90      CONTINUE                                                 6500
C...   NO PERMITTED DELIMITER FOUND. TRY NEXT POSITION               6510
            GO TO 70                                                 6520
C...   FOLLOWING DELIMITERS                                          6530
   100      K = MDEL2(MFEAT,1)                                       6540
            IF ((JPT + J) .GE. IPT .OR. K .EQ. 0) GO TO 120          6550
C...   CHECK THROUGH DELIMITER SET                                   6560
            K = K + 1                                                6570
            II = JPT + J + 1                                         6580
            II = MREF(II)                                            6590
            DO 110 I = 2, K                                          6600
            IF (II .EQ. MDEL2(MFEAT,I)) GO TO 120                    6610
   110      CONTINUE                                                 6620
C...   NO PERMITTED DELIMITER. TRY NEXT POSITION                     6630
            GO TO 70                                                 6640
```

Fig. 5.3A — Part of a tidied Fortran program listing.

of written information about the program which can augment any existing documentation or make up for its absence. All this new information, together with new descriptions of the program and any other notes which may help in its understanding, should be collated and added to the documentation file, so that it may provide help if the program is later taken over by yet another person who must again try to understand its working.

It is clear from the previous discussion that understanding other people's programs may require considerable effort. If the program is complex and the documentation is poor, then it is possible that the effort needed to read and understand it sufficiently well to maintain and modify it, is greater than the effort needed to write a new program to the same specification. In these circumstances it may well be sensible to abandon the original program. This reflects badly on the program's designers and authors, and thus provides a salutory example for those who would write its replacement. The decision to abandon and re-write may, however, not be yours.

Program maintenance

There are two main reasons for the maintenance of computer programs. The first is a consequence of our inability to write large programs which are completely free of all errors; that is, the location and correction of program bugs. The detection of errors is a process which, in many cases, continues throughout the lifetime of the program. The majority of the errors are uncovered and corrected during the formal process of debugging and testing, before the program is considered to be finished. A further smaller crop will be harvested during the early life of the program, when it is used with real data, which may be less predictable than the test data. Usually the original programmer or programming team is still accessible, and can be used to clear these errors. The problems start later, when an error occurs in an established program. The difficulties are compounded because the cause of an error which has lain dormant for a long time is likely to be difficult to find.

The second reason is the modification of existing programs to meet changed specifications. Programs must be altered to satisfy changing users' needs, and to incorporate improvements. In an academic environment it is common practice to cannibalize existing programs for modules which can then be used in the construction of new programs. Some adaptation of these modules may be necessary to make them fit the changed circumstances.

Both cases require the programmer to acquire a general understanding of the whole program, and an understanding, in depth, of those parts which are to be corrected or modified. Where an existing program has shown up an error, this deep understanding is particularly necessary to ascertain precisely what is wrong and what must be done to set it right. In both cases, care must be taken to ensure that the changes are made without disturbing the rest of the program and so introducing other errors or unwanted side effects. This is sometimes called the spaghetti problem. A badly structured program is likened to a plateful of spaghetti: if one strand is pulled, then the ramifications can be seen at the other side of the plate where there is mysterious turbulence and upheaval. The spaghetti effect in programs without a modular structure can often be traced to variables which are used for more than one purpose in otherwise separate parts of the program. Potential trouble spots can be identified from the variable directory table. Another frequent cause is the use of long-distance conditional branch or goto instructions, which may transfer control round the program at a speed which exceeds the programmer's comprehension. Because structured programming controls both the scope of variables and the program flow, the spaghetti effect is minimal or absent in programs written under this discipline. (See Section 2.4.)

Mention has already been made of the effect that program style has on the ease of understanding. Each programmer tends to write in his own idiosyncratic style, and so, unless a conscious effort is made to follow the existing style, there is a very real risk that the modified program will become 'schizophrenic'; that it will exhibit two or more different styles. This will make it more difficult to understand in the future. The maintenance programmer should be aware of, and guard against, this possibility.

The process of understanding is beset with possibilities for misunderstanding, and that of modification with possibilities for error. Hence there is a good chance that one or more new bugs will have been introduced into the program during modification. The modified program must be thoroughly tested to eliminate this possibility and to verify that it does indeed function according to its specification. The original set of test procedures and data should form the basis for this testing, but are not by themselves sufficient. If the modification was carried out to correct a previously undetected error, then it may be assumed that the original testing did not uncover the error. It will not, therefore, check that it has been corrected satisfactorily. Additional tests must be designed to verify the correction; the program must pass both these, and the original tests. Modifications which have changed the program to meet a changed specification, will have invalidated part or all of the original test set. New tests, which may include relevant parts of the old tests, must now be devised. Program testing and debugging is discussed in Section 3.2.

It should be unnecessary to add that the program documentation must be changed in step with the program itself. Documentation is useful only if kept up to date, and documentation which refers to a previous version of the program may be gravely misleading. The program documentation should be amended to show the change: what was changed, why it was changed, when it was changed, who changed it, and how the program now functions. The source code should also be annotated with comments to show that a change has been made, including brief details as to why, what, when, and who.

Portability

Despite many good intentions proclaimed over the years by computer manufacturers, and learned papers on portability by software specialists, it is still a
troublesome and often expensive task to move a program from one machine to
another. Problems can, and often do, occur even when the transfer is between
two machines from a single manufacturer, or between two identical machines
running under different operating systems. The uncertainty may be reduced,
although not eliminated, if the program is originally designed and written with
portability in mind. Generally this means writing in a high-level language and,
moreover, rigid adherence to some proven portability standard. The transfer of
programs written in an assembler language is possible, but usually only with
the extensive use of automatic conversion aids such as macroprocessors. The
implications of portability on the selection of a programming language are
discussed in Sections 2.1 and 2.2.

Program transfer may be regarded as a form of total modification, and
indeed, much of the philosophy of the preceding subsection is applicable. The
programmer should develop a general understanding of the whole program and
take care that any changes which may be necessary do not result in a spaghetti
effect. The transferred program must be tested exhaustively, if possible by using
the original test set so that the original tests are replicated. Code passages which
have been changed in the transfer process deserve special attention, and so the
tests of the resulting program should be at least as searching as the tests of the
original. Finally, the transfer must be documented. Here again, areas which have
been changed should be detailed. Only when it is certain beyond reasonable
doubt that the two programs − before and after the transfer − are functionally
equivalent, should any further modifications be made.

Six broad problem areas may be identified in this connection:
- language differences;
- representation of variables;
- file handling;
- special peripheral handling;
- program size and execution speed;
- operating system interface.

Language differences and deviations from the standards were discussed in
Section 2.2. Clearly, they present a problem that will remain with us for some
time. Fortunately, systematic differences are relatively easily detected, and once
found, may be systematically changed. This tedious and exacting task can, in
some cases, be helped by the use of a macroprocessor to make mechanical
amendments. The macroprocessor complements the programmer, but cannot
provide a complete solution by itself, because this would require intelligence
beyond the reach of the program.

Similarly, the problems of representation of variables were covered in
Section 2.2. In the case of character handling, for instance, the different repre-

sentation may require alteration of the program logic to detect special characters and allow for a different collating sequence — that is, ordering of the characters. Changes of this sort would have to be made manually and extremely carefully. Where systematic changes such as non-standard representations of constants (for example, octal and hexadecimal) have to be made, again the use of a macro-processor is usually practicable.

Perhaps the most elusive and difficult transfer problem, especially in numerical algorithms, is posed by different representations of real variables. These give rise to different ranges and to different accuracies. The accumulation of errors, due to the internal binary representation, during a sequence of calculations is alarming and, if the accuracy is low and the calculations are complex, then the accumulation may be catastrophic. Sometimes the calculation errors resulting from inaccurate representation may pass unnoticed, masked by inadequate testing, until the program is transferred to a more accurate machine. The accuracy also determines the smallest number which may be distinguished from zero. The obvious problem areas include the inversion of matrices and integration, where the algorithms used must be chosen with care for their sensitivity. It is worth noting here that iterative techniques are relatively free from accuracy problems. The only precautions which can be taken are, firstly to understand the numerical algorithms used and to carry out some error anaylsis before transferring the program, and secondly to test the program exhaustively both before and after the transfer, using carefully prepared data. The remedy may be found by using double precision or long variables in sensitive computations, or by the use of more accurate or stable algorithms.

Different implementations of languages, running under different operating systems, vary in their method of and ability in handling external files. In some cases files are associated with the program by the operating system via the job control language, while in others a special program segment or procedure is used to define the interface between the program and its external files. If the program uses random access files, it will be difficult to transfer it to a system that does not support the facility, even though it may be available on the hardware. Often the only efficient solution is to rewrite the program.

Programs which use special peripherals, like graphic terminals or optical character readers, are similarly vexing. The peripheral may depend on special control codes which cannot be generated, or are ignored or deleted by the new system or cause errors in it. Frequently, identical peripherals are not available on the new system, and so the program must be modified to produce different output sequences or to accept different inputs. The difficulties are minimized, or at least localized, if the program was originally written with separate peripheral handling procedures.

If the program is large or runs for a long time on a powerful computer, it may be impracticable to run it on a slower or smaller machine, without extensive optimization. This is discussed in Sections 3.3, 4.2, and 4.3.

Operating systems offer a selection of idiosyncratic facilities, enabling programs to communicate with the outside world, and in some instances, to monitor their performance, trapping exception conditions and invoking system routines. There are no general rules for this area of conversion; each instance must be considered and dealt with separately.

This catalogue of possible problems associated with program transfer and their tedious and time-consuming solutions makes depressing reading. Happily, it is only rarely that all the problems occur in the transfer of any one program. However, they should all be considered, during the process that can be termed the design of the transfer. It this is done, it will be possible to come to an informed opinion of the effort that will be required, and then take the decision on whether to transfer, or to rewrite.

Not only the problems associated with the transfer of programs, but all those discussed in this section — ease of readability, ease of maintenance, ease of updating — should be at the back of your mind when writing a program. Yours might be 'another person's program' one day in the future.

Nick Rushby

5.4 WORKING AS ONE OF A TEAM

The use of techniques and standards which assist in successful design and implementation of computer programs, discussed throughout this book, becomes very evident when the development effort required to implement a computer project is too great for one person. In such cases, it is necessary to form a project team. This section considers the role of an individual within such a team.

Software development projects involving more than one person have historically been conducted mainly in the commercial environment, where tight control of development methods and timescale is essential. However, the scale and complexity of projects being undertaken within university and research environments is constantly increasing, resulting in the formation of project teams for particular tasks. While the timescale for such projects may not be as severe as in the commercial environment, the standards to be applied, and the roles of individuals within the project, remain the same. It is particularly advantageous for undergraduate students to work on a project with other people at some stage on their degree course. The lessons learned and the habits gained can provide useful experience for later employment, whereas bad habits formed early can prove difficult to overcome.

Role of the individual
The most important rule for development projects requiring more than one person is that the project *must* have a structure. Each individual working on the project must be aware of his exact role and responsibilities within the project, and the objectives he is trying to achieve. There is a temptation with smaller

projects, particularly where there is little formal supervision, to attempt to run the project as a programming commune, with responsibilities shared between members of the team on an ad hoc basis. This approach does not work. Effort becomes duplicated in some areas and not applied in others, and there is a tendency for people to work on those parts of the project which interest them most, ignoring the less interesting parts without which the project can never be finished. The result is usually a project two-thirds completed, and no-one interested in finishing the remaining work.

Inherent in the concept of a project structure is the requirement that there must be a project leader; that is, someone who has overall responsibility for the ultimate completion of the entire project. It is essential that one person has the responsibility to decide how, when, and by whom each part of the project is implemented. This person may either be someone working full-time as a member of the project team, or may be a supervisor or manager with responsibility for other concurrently-running projects. In either case, the project leader must define the role of each individual within the project. (The role of project leader is discussed later in this section.) Each individual is then responsible for completion of the tasks allocated to him.

Before starting work on a project, each member of the team must be able to resolve several questions:

1. Are the objectives clear?

    Each person must ensure that he is fully aware of what he is attempting to achieve. If he is responsible for development of a self-contained portion of the project, the objective is probably fairly clear. If, however, he is developing a portion in conjunction with one or more other members of the team, he must ensure both that there is no overlapping of responsibilities which will cause duplication of effort, and conversely, that none of the workload is left unallocated. If the objectives are not clear, the individual must ask the project leader, for nothing inhibits progress more than uncertainty.

2. Are the resources available?

    To complete the allocated task, each individual will require certain resources. These resources may range from data preparation facilities, for example card-punching requirements, to machine time requirements, for example access to a terminal or a computer. Assistance from other people may be required at various stages of development, or a particular software package may need to be available. It is the responsibility of each individual to think ahead and ensure that all the facilities he will require to complete the task are available, or can be made available at the appropriate time.

3. Can the timescale be met?

    Every task to be accomplished must have a timescale associated with it. The timescale may be limited by the necessity to complete the entire project within a certain elapsed time or, for an intermediate step, to use the completed facility to develop a further stage of the project. When a portion of work has been allocated, the individual must ensure that sufficient time is available to complete the tasks. Some timescales in a project will be tight and some will be generous; it is not always possible to produce an optimal development schedule, because of external constraints such as hardware availability or a fixed completion date. If the timescale is generous, it is best to aim to complete the task a little ahead of schedule. This allows for unexpected problems or delays that may appear later, and assists in speeding the overall development of the project (not to mention your own reputation in the eyes of your superior!). If the timescale is tight, think carefully, before you start, whether it is reasonable to expect to finish the task in the time available. There is likely to be very little margin for error, so ensure that you are fully aware of the scope of the task, and plan your work accordingly. It is pointless to begin a task knowing that the deadline given cannot possibly be met; it is far better to tell the project leader that the timescale is too tight and ask for an extension. You will, of course, have to explain your reasons! Project leaders welcome such feedback, since it is much easier to replan or to reallocate resources during the earlier stages of a project.

The questions mentioned above help to outline the requirements and demands of each individual on a project. (Indeed, they are also necessary when an individual undertakes a project on his own.) Having agreed to undertake a particular task, knowing what is to be done, knowing what resources are required, and knowing how long he has to complete the task, the individual then takes responsibility for the work. In so doing, he also takes on responsibilities to the other members of the team. Having made his demands on the project, he must make every effort to work within the demands of the project. It is these demands, and the individual's ability to respond to them, that determine his usefulness — or otherwise — to the project.

When an individual develops a program as a single entity on his own, he has almost total freedom on the methods he adopts. (In fact, it is this freedom which often results in a very poor end product.) When an individual works within a team, however, he no longer has such freedom, and must learn to work within certain constraints. These constraints are placed on him only as a necessity, not as an imposition, and paradoxically, within these constraints, he may have more freedom to produce a better quality product. The constraints can be summed up as a need for the individual to be aware of the requirements of (a) the other members of the team, (b) the project leader, and (c) the users who will make use of the completed product. If he can satisfy these three sets of people, he will have performed his role within the project successfully.

The first constraint, and perhaps the most important, is that of documentation. The subject of documentation has been discussed in detail in Section 5.1, but it is the application of this requirement that most separates the amateur from the professional programmer. The amateur avoids documentation: his argument usually runs on the lines of 'I understand the program, therefore I know how to change it, and besides, no-one will ever read the documentation'. The professional programmer, on the other hand, appreciates that writing and maintaining documentation is as vital as writing and maintaining the program itself. He knows that other people will want to understand and perhaps enhance the program, and that his documentation must enable the program to be easily understood. Without this approach, it is not possible to work within a team.

Each project will have a documentation standard, and it is the responsibility of each member of the project to adhere to that standard. As a project develops, the role of individuals may change, because of illness, promotion, or someone leaving, and it must therefore be possible for another person to take over development of a program should this be required. In addition, the project leader may need to audit the overall system design, and the eventual users of the system may want to study individual programs with a view to maintenance and enhancement. Accordingly, all programs within a project must be developed to a common standard. The particular standard adopted is not all that important, as long as people consider it informative and not too constraining.

The use of comments on program listings should be considered part of the documentation standard, as these provide a useful reference for anyone attempting to follow the design of a program. Other members of the project will almost certainly need to look at each individual's program at some stage, either to desk-check it (see Section 5.2), or to attempt to solve a complex error during system integration. It is the responsibility of each programmer to adhere to the appropriate documentation standards and to update his documentation when required.

A second constraint is in the use of computer time. Several people concurrently attempting to implement a number of programs on a single computer tend to produce a total requirement for testing facilities which exceeds the available computer time. While this constraint may not be so evident in the research environment, it is always present in the commercial environment. It is therefore a valuable asset, as a team member, to learn to limit the total computer time required to test a program thoroughly.

Many people, while learning to program, consider that they are testing only when the program is running in the computer. (This attitude is often a result of the almost unlimited machine time available at some universities.) More-experienced programmers learn that testing a program can be more efficient when most of the work is carried out offline. Offline testing can take several forms. Firstly, the program can be desk-checked as thoroughly as possible, preferably with the assistance of another member of the team. Secondly, before beginning the test run, the programmer can consider carefully what he is trying to achieve during the run, what results he expects to see, and what information he will want to monitor during and after the run. It is totally wrong to approach a test run intending to run one subsection of a program and 'seeing what happens', since this results in considerable time being spent at the computer analysing where the program went wrong. It is this 'thinking time' which should be kept offline as much as possible. By preparing each test run thoroughly, it should be possible in most cases to set up and run the program and output the test results very quickly — say, in no more than about twenty minutes, though this is obviously somewhat system-dependent. Analysis of the output is thus done offline, and the computer is available for others to use.

The difficulty of access to computer time for several individuals without a time-sharing facility can be greatly resolved if each person adopts a testing philosophy as outlined above. As a last resort, a booking system for allocating computer time may have to be introduced, but even with such a system it is advisable to keep the individual booking time as short as possible, say one hour maximum. This encourages individuals to test offline as much as possible, and reduces disagreements about the allocation of computer time. Each individual within the project has the responsibility of ensuring that he does not use more than a reasonable share of the available computer resources.

A third constraint is the work allocated to each individual. Within any project, some work is more interesting than other parts. Each person must be prepared to take responsibility for some of the less interesting work, since the total project cannot be finished until all parts have been completed. It is best to view this type of work as a challenge, to be completed as quickly and effectively as possible, and to resist the temptation to leave the work until the last possible moment, when it will surely be completed hurriedly, and usually badly. In general, each programmer should make every effort to meet the timescale for each portion of work, without especially favouring the most interesting technical aspects.

Lastly, it is extremely important that each programmer discusses his work with other team members (see Section 3.1). Discussion often provokes new ideas, and is one of the best methods for solving stubborn system faults. A new mind applied to an old problem can often produce results. There is an unfortunate side effect to this, however, which is sometimes prevalent in less-experienced programmers. Having been given total responsibility for a program, they feel it is up to them, and them alone, to solve all problems associated with that program. They resist outside assistance, and discourage discussion of their program; they feel threatened, and that in some way they have become less important, and are no longer the authority on their own area of work. This attitude is totally unnecessary, however, and within a project environment it can be counter-productive. The role of each program has to be discussed with other team members, but no-one ever knows the working of a particular program better than the person who wrote it. His knowledge will always remain vital to the project. Each programmer must develop the self-confidence to discuss his work freely and allow other people to suggest alterations to the design of his program (he can, after all, equally well suggest alterations to other people's programs). It is only through the discussion of technical problems that development can eventually succeed.

A further consideration must be the relationship with the project leader. He may be subject to severe outside constraints in the manner in which the project is implemented, and may not be able to offer the exact type of work or timescale each individual would like. However, having agreed to undertake a particular task, each programmer must support the project leader in meeting his targets. Especially on a large project, the project leader will not be able to devote much of his time to the detailed monitoring of the technical progress of each individual in the team. Most programmers prefer not to be too closely monitored as to their daily progress, but this freedom in turn produces a responsibility on the part of each one to inform the project leader of any problems that are likely to impede his progress. If it becomes no longer possible to meet the timescale, he must inform the project leader as soon as possible so that steps can be taken to rectify the position. Early action can save a lot of time later, but pretending to be able to meet the timescale when it is obviously impracticable only causes longer delays at a later stage in the project.

Leading a team yourself

Many people graduate to team leadership after considerable experience of working within project teams, and consequently retain a considerable interest in the technical aspects of the project. While it is highly desirable that the project leader has sufficient technical experience to estimate and plan the development effort, he must avoid the mistake of becoming so involved in the technical problems of implementation that he is unable to devote sufficient time to the management of the project. The correct division of his time between management and technical work will depend on several factors, for example the size of the project, the range of experience of other project members, and the environment in which the project is being run. In a small project of two or three people, the project leader's role will probably be mainly technical, perhaps as the overall system designer, but a large project of 15 to 20 people will require a full-time project *manager*. As a guideline, the project leader should aim to undertake slightly less technical work than he considers himself able to achieve. In particular, he should not undertake a development task which is on the project critical path. If any unforeseen management problem arises, it will be his responsibility to resolve that problem as his main priority; his development work will suffer, and the project timescale will suffer as a result. It is far preferable that the project leader should undertake those technical tasks on a project which do not involve program development, for example production of the functional specification, or definition of acceptance tests. These tasks are more interruptable in the event of unexpected problems arising, and tend to have a longer and more involved schedule for production, often requiring interaction with the end user.

On many projects, the role of the project leader changes throughout the duration of the project. It is quite common that his early role is mainly technical, perhaps analysing the overall definition of the project; but as the implementation gathers momentum, he gradually delegates the detailed technical decisions to the senior members of the team who have been engaged in the system design, while he himself becomes increasingly involved in the overall management of the project. The extent of this change in role will depend very much on the size of the project.

A typical software development project has several distinct phases, as follows:

1. Functional specification

    Defining precisely all the functions to be performed by the system, in as much detail as possible.

2. System design

    Designing all software required to perform the functions described in the functional specification.

3. Program specification

    Specifying and documenting all programs, program interfaces, and data structures required.

4. Coding

    Writing the individual program modules.

5. Module testing

    Compiling, assembling, and testing each individual program module.

6. System integration

    Building the individual modules into a trusted system.

7. Acceptance tests

    Running a series of tests to demonstrate that the system performs the functions described in the functional specification.

8. Commissioning

    Installing the completed system on the user's premises, with possible enhancements to the software.

9. Final documentation

    Updating all program documentation to reflect the final version of the software system.

A well-run project will move smoothly from one phase to the next, with minimal requirement for feedback into a previous phase. With a badly-run project, on the other hand, it is not always clear where one phase ends and the next begins. It is the responsibility of the project leader to maintain the progress of the project through each phase. Wherever possible, the project leader should aim to be the first person to start work on the project. He is thus able to develop a sound estimate of the size of the overall development required, and can then determine and organize the roles of other members of the project effectively. It is extremely difficult to join a project midway as a project leader and still be able to lead a team effectively, since other members are further advanced in their understanding of the system.

Assuming, then, that the project leader has started work before the other members of the project, what are his main responsibilities? He must attempt to provide the proper environment within which the other members can work; this environment has been outlined in the previous part of this section. Each individual's role must be clear, with well-defined objectives and responsibilities. He must ensure that all tasks are included in the project plan, and that each task is ultimately the responsibility of one person. To achieve this, he should attempt to think a little wider and further than other members of the project. In particular, items like test and debugging software, modification of existing packages, and user documentation are often overlooked at the planning stage, yet can entail significant development effort during the project.

Allocating tasks to particular individuals should be done with considerable care. Different people have interests in different areas of software development, and it is helpful to allocate a particular task to the person likely to be most interested in developing that task. A useful guide here is the person's experience. What type of work has he done in the past? His role should enable him to use this experience, and yet should present some challenge to develop that experience more broadly. In this way, the individual is stretched to achieve the objectives, but has sufficient experience to know how to undertake the task. If the responsibility for the completion of the task is now delegated totally to the individual, subject to the requirement to report progress regularly, the combination of responsibility, challenge, and confidence based on experience offers the individual a real measure of job satisfaction, which should motivate him to work positively to meet the timescale.

Delegation of authority is always difficult, and the fault frequently lies with the delegator. Too often the task is 'delegated', but the project leader insists on retaining too close a control over the implementation of the task. This is particularly inadvisable with program development, which to some extent always reflects the style of the programmer, and in general it is best to allow the programmer as much freedom as possible to implement the design in his own manner. If the overall system design is sound, and the program interfaces are clearly defined, an exact method for individual implementation is not essential.

In addition to specifying the role of each individual, the project leader must estimate the time required to complete every task. Estimating timescales is one of the most difficult tasks for any project leader, and many projects which finish late do so because the total effort required had been grossly underestimated at the start of the project. There is no golden rule to assist estimating; experience in program development is the best ally. Estimating the total effort for a large amount of work can be made more accurate by estimating the effort required for each portion of the work. The smaller each portion, the more accurate the total estimate will be, as the errors tend to average out rather than increase when totalled. One thing you can be sure of, though — everything will take much longer than you think! People often underestimate the total time taken because they consider only the time taken to write the program. In practice, the coding time is a small fraction of the total time required. A program must be designed, specified, coded, tested, integrated with other programs, possibly even commissioned on a user's site, and of course documented. A development rate of 10 to 20 statements per day, or 10 to 20 words of assembler program per day, is a realistic estimate of the *total* effort required to develop a program. The experience of the programmer, the development facilities available, and the complexity of the code all affect the rate of production. Poor editing, assembling, or debugging facilities, and slow job turn-round times can all delay progress significantly, and an intricate systems program is far slower to develop than a simple file update program.

Having estimated each task on the project, and allocated the work fairly across the project team, the project leader must define the standards to be used throughout the project. These standards should include:
— documentation standards
— programming standards
— reporting standards.

Documentation standards have been discussed in earlier sections. Programming standards should specify any programming conventions that must be used (or avoided), and the layout of program listings with their associated comments. All flow charts should be drawn to a common convention, for ease of understanding. Reporting standards should specify how, when, and to whom each individual should report progress. Exactly which standards are chosen is not so important, but it is vitally important that they are enforced across the project team. Standards provide a framework within which a project can work, but without such standards it is not possible to develop a project successfully.

Throughout the duration of a project, the project leader must monitor closely the progress of each individual. He should aim to delegate each task fully, yet retain close control over the execution of the task. This is a narrow path which must be trodden carefully. With too tight a control, the task does not appear to the individual as fully delegated; insufficient control results in the project leader being unable to respond quickly enough if a task is behind schedule. It is best to hold regular progress meetings, say once a month, at which progress can be reviewed, current problems pinpointed, and likely future problems anticipated; in between, allow people as much freedom as possible to complete their tasks by themselves. One other idea to measure overall progress, and to discover any hidden bottlenecks, is to hold a 'technical run-through', where programs are verbally 'run-through' in sequence by each individual to demonstrate the flow of information through and between programs. A forum of this kind often exposes outstanding design faults and weaknesses in particular programs. A word of warning here, however. It is easy to get into the habit of holding meetings too often, and meetings often give the impression of progress when in fact little is being achieved. A lot of productive man-hours can be tied up in meetings, and for technical problems this is not an effective development method. In general, technical meetings should be limited to those who are most concerned with the particular subject under discussion.

The final consideration regarding project leadership may appear obvious, but is too often disregarded. A project leader must at all times strive to work *with* his team. People will respect you for your ability, not for your position. Ivory tower leadership never really works anywhere, but it is particularly inappropriate with computer projects. Programmers are strongly self-motivated, and respond well to good guidance, but resent an authoritative style of leadership. The project leader should attempt to lead by example, efficiency, and involvement with his team. The goal of the entire team should be the same — to complete the development within the timescale, and in a professional manner. A good project leader brings out the best in his team, and a good team can achieve an end product that exceeds the contribution of each individual.

Project work is among the most stimulating and creative work to be found anywhere, and the greater the contribution of each individual, the greater the rewards and satisfaction that each will obtain. A good project has an identity and a style of its own, and is remembered by those who worked on it long after the project has ceased to exist. If, in addition, the end product has real permanence and considerable functional value to society, there is surely little more one can ask from a career.

Martin Wilson

References and Further Reading

GENERAL

Detailed and exhaustive coverage of the subject can be found in

  J. D. Aron, *The program development process,* Addison-Wesley, 1974
which is worth consulting, as is the book by Weinberg cited under Chapter 5
below. A useful guide to the literature is provided by

  T. Anderson and S. K. Shrivastava, Reliable software: a selective annotated
  bibliography, *Software Practice and Experience,* **8**, pp 59-76, 1978.

CHAPTER 1

Among books concerned with the design of algorithms,

  N. Wirth, *Algorithms + Data Structures = Programs,* Prentice-Hall, 1976
can certainly be recommended, as can

  S. Alagic and M. A. Arbib, *The design of well-structured and correct programs,*
  Springer-Verlag, 1978
although the title hides the fact that a good deal of it is devoted to programming
in Pascal. A major source of algorithms is

  D. E. Knuth, *The art of computer programming,* Addison-Wesley,
a projected set of seven volumes of which at the time of writing the following
have appeared:

  Vol. 1 *Fundamental algorithms* (2nd ed. 1974);

  Vol. 2 *Semi-numerical algorithms* (2nd ed. 1978);

  Vol. 3 *Sorting and searching* (1972).

CHAPTER 2

On questions concerning the choice of programming language (Section 2.1),
the following books can be consulted:

  D. W. Barron, *An introduction to the study of programming languages,*
  Cambridge U. P. 1977;

B. Higman, *A comparative study of programming languages,* MacDonald and Janes, 2nd ed. 1977;

B. L. Meek, *Fortran, PL/I and the Algols,* Macmillan, 1978;

J. E. Nicholls, *The structure and design of programming languages,* Addison-Wesley, 1975;

W. W. Peterson, *Introduction to programming languages,* Prentice-Hall, 1974;

A. B. Tucker Jr., *Programming Languages,* McGraw-Hill, 1977.

For more discussion of Fortran standards and transferability, see

A. C. Day, *Compatible Fortran,* Cambridge University Press, 1978;

D. T. Muxworthy, *A review of program portability and Fortran conventions,* European Computer Program Institute, 1976;

S. Summers and J. Fox, Writing machine independent Fortran, *Software World,* **9**, No. 2, 1978.

The literature on structured programming is now extensive, and most books on programming written since the appearance of

O. J. Dahl, E. W. Dijkstra and C. A. R. Hoare, *Structured Programming,* Academic Press, 1972

embody its principles or at least pay lip-service to them. The full references of the papers cited in Section 2.4 are

P. Naur, Goto statements and good Algol style, *BIT* **3**, 204–5, 1963; and

E. W. Dijkstra, GOTO statement considered harmful, *Communications of the A. C. M.* **11**, 147–8, 1968.

The paper cited above by Anderson and Shrivastava includes a section on *Programming methodology* which gives further references including

M. A. Jackson, *Principles of program design,* Academic Press, 1975;

B. W. Kernighan and P. J. Plauger, *The elements of programming style,* McGraw-Hill, 1974;

B. W. Kernighan and P. J. Plauger, *Software tools,* Addison-Wesley, 1976;

E. W. Dijkstra, *A discipline of programming,* Prentice-Hall, 1976;

N. Wirth, *Systematic programming: an introduction,* Prentice-Hall, 1973;

all of which are recommended. See also

Structured programming, *Infotech State of the Art Report,* 1974.

The two examples in Section 2.4 are taken from

P. Naur *et al, Revised Report on the algorithmic language Algol 60* (1962)

extensively reprinted in many books and journals, but see for example *Computer Journal* **5**, 349–67, 1963; and

M. J. R. Healy, Algorithm AS 7: inversion of a positive semi-definite symmetric matrix, *Applied Statistics* **17**, 198–99, 1968.

CHAPTER 3

The following are recommended for further reading:

A. R. Brown and W. A. Sampson, *Program debugging,* MacDonald, 1973;

Central Computer Agency, *Program validation,* H. M. S. O., 1976;

R. Rustin (ed.) *Debugging techniques in large systems,* Prentice-Hall 1971;

D. Van Tassel, *Program style, design, efficiency, debugging and testing,* Prentice-Hall, 1974;

S. Lauesan, Debugging Techniques, *Software Practice and Experience,* **9,** 51–64, 1979.

See also the section on *Software certification* in Anderson and Shrivastava, *op. cit.*

CHAPTER 4

On heuristic programming (Section 4.1), from the very large number of possible references, many dealing with specific problems, we have chosen two elementary textbooks:

E. M. Rheingold, J. Nievergelt and N. Deo, *Combinatorial Algorithms,* Prentice-Hall, 1976;

N. J. Nilsson, *Problem-solving methods in artificial intelligence,* McGraw-Hill, 1971;

and two more advanced review papers:

R. Kowalski, *AND/OR* graphs, *theorem-proving graphs and bi-directional search,* in B. Meltzer and D. Michie (eds), *Machine intelligence 5,* Edinburgh University Press, 1972, 167–194;

I. Pohl, *Considerations in heuristic search algorithms,* in E. Elcock and D. Michie (eds), *Machine intelligence 8,* Ellis Horwood, 1977, 55–72.

On the later sections, the following are recommended for further reading:

S. J. Waters, *Introduction to computer systems design,* National Computing Centre, 1973;

J. Martin, *Design of real-time computer systems,* Prentice-Hall, 1967;

INFOTECH *State of the Art Report No. 3: Real Time,* Infotech Limited, 1971;

G. M. Bull and S. F. G. Packham, *Time Sharing Systems,* McGraw Hill, 1971;

R. Watson, *Time Sharing Design Concepts,* McGraw Hill, 1970;

R. C. Turner, *Real-time programming with microprocessors,* Lexington, 1979;

Introduction to Real Time, International Computers Ltd, 1971;

H. Lorin, *Parallelism in Hardware and Software: Real and Apparent Concurrency,* Prentice-Hall, 1971;

Open University TM221 Course team, *Event-controlled input-output; the minicomputer in a laboratory,* Open University, TM221 units 10–11, 1975; and also other TM221 units. The paper mentioned Section 4.2 is

I. S. Duff: A survey of sparse matrix research, *Proc. IEEE* **65,** 500–535, 1977.

CHAPTER 5

Good guidelines for documentation of all kinds, including sotftware, are laid down in:

G. Mellor and J. G. Rickerby, *Data processing documentation standards,* National Computing Centre, 1977.

See also

J. D. Lomax, *Documentation of software products,* National Computing Centre, 1977;

R. W. Witty, Dimensional flowcharting, *Software Practice and Experience* 7, 553–584, 1977;

R. S. Scowen, Some aids for program documentation, *Software Practice and Experience* 7, 779–792, 1977.

The book cited in Section 5.1 is

H. D. Leeds and G. M. Weinberg, *Computer programming fundamentals,* McGraw-Hill 1966.

On program portability (Section 5.3), see the items on specific languages cited under Chapter 2 above, and also

P. J. Brown, *Macroprocessors and techniques for portable software,* Wiley, 1974;

J. F. Fleiss, G. W. Phillips, A. Edwards and L. Reider, *Programming for transferability,* International Computer Systems Inc., 1972;

A. S. Tanenbaum, P. Klint, and W. Bohm, Guidelines for software portability *Software Practice and Experience* 8, 681–698, 1978.

For discussion of (and many entertaining and enlightening examples of) many of the problems discussed in this book, but those of working with other people (Section 5.4) in particular, see

G. H. Weinberg, *The psychology of computer programming,* Van Nostrand, 1971.

Also well worth reading is

F. P. Brooks, *The mythical man-month,* Addison-Wesley 1974.

Index